The Pony Club

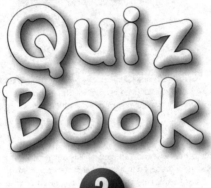

Quiz Book

2

The Pony Club
Stoneleigh Park
Kenilworth
Warwickshire
CV8 2RW

Website: www.pcuk.org

Published in the UK by The Pony Club

© 2011 The Pony Club

First published in 2002

British Library Cataloguing-in-Publication Data
A catalogue record for this book
is available from the British Library.

ISBN 978–1–907279–09–6

Compiled by Judith Draper

Designed and produced for
The Pony Club by Paul Harding

Printed in Great Britain by Halstan & Co.

Trade distribution by Kenilworth Press
An imprint of Quiller Publishing Ltd.
Wykey House, Wykey, Shrewsbury, SY4 1JA
Tel: 01939 261616 Fax: 01939 261606
Email: info@quillerbooks.com
Website: www.kenilworthpress.co.uk

Contents

QUESTIONS

ANSWERS

? Take Your Pick

1   Which novel by Anna
    Sewell became a
    worldwide best seller?
    [a] *Black Riders*
    [b] *Black Beauty*
    [c] *The Black Tulip*

2   Which of these British
    native pony breeds is
    the smallest?
    [a] Dartmoor
    [b] Highland
    [c] Shetland

3   Where do the finals of
    the Pony Club Mounted
    Games Championships
    take place?
    [a] NEC, Birmingham
    [b] Olympia
    [c] Hickstead

4   Where would you
    expect to find an
    eggbutt snaffle?
    [a] In a kitchen
    [b] In a chicken run
    [c] In a horse's mouth

5   Which part of a horse
    or pony is usually
    affected by mud fever?
    [a] The head
    [b] The neck
    [c] The legs

6   In which equestrian
    sport do horses
    perform a half-pass?
    [a] Polo
    [b] Dressage
    [c] Racing

7   Where on a saddle
    is the cantle?
    [a] Underneath
    [b] At the back
    [c] At the front

8   What does a 'nappy'
    horse do?
    [a] Sleeps most of the
        day
    [b] Bites its handler
    [c] Refuses to do what
        its rider asks

9   In which continent
    would you find
    'wild' Mustang
    horses?
    [a] South America
    [b] North America
    [c] Asia

10 Where on a pony is 'the
    white line'?
    [a] On his face
    [b] Along his back
    [c] In his hoof

11 **What are 'brasses'?**
[a] Candlesticks
[b] Ornaments for draught horses
[c] Musical instruments used by mounted bands

12 **What is an Atherstone?**
[a] A cricketer
[b] A sharpening tool
[c] A girth

13 **On what did Queen Elizabeth I ride?**
[a] A palfrey
[b] A palanquin
[c] A pallet

14 **What is a quiddor?**
[a] A horse who 'naps'
[b] A horse who drops food from his mouth while eating
[c] A horse who fetches a small price at auction

15 **How many beats per minute is the horse's normal pulse rate?**
[a] 30–35
[b] 35–40
[c] 40–45

16 **Which stud book is divided into sections A, B, C and D?**
[a] *The General Stud Book*
[b] *The Welsh Pony and Cob Society Stud Book*
[c] *The Hackney Horse Society Stud Book*

17 **What is a horsemaster?**
[a] Someone who teaches horses tricks
[b] Someone who knows all about horse care
[c] Someone who organises horse shows

18 **What is a 'blood horse'?**
[a] A Thoroughbred
[b] A lightweight hunter
[c] An Arabian

19 **What is a quarter clip?**
[a] Part of a horseshoe
[b] A type of trace clip
[c] A slow gallop

20 **What is a plug?**
[a] A 'horse for sale' notice in a local newspaper
[b] A worthless, common horse
[c] A horseshoe nail

21 Where does the Barb horse come from?
[a] Arabia
[b] North Africa
[c] Spain

22 If two colts are by different stallions but out of the same mare, what is their relationship?
[a] Full brothers
[b] Half brothers
[c] Technically no relationship at all

23 What is the English translation of the French term *renvers*?
[a] Quarters-out
[b] Quarters-in
[c] Rein-back

24 What is a Tarpan?
[a] A cross between a donkey and an Andalusian horse
[b] A storage box situated beneath a carriage driver's seat
[c] A breed of wild horse believed to be an ancestor of the modern horse

25 What kind of laugh is a 'horse laugh'?
[a] Cheerful
[b] High-pitched
[c] Coarse and vulgar

26 What is a bosal?
[a] A type of horse bred in Bosnia
[b] A type of bitless bridle
[c] A type of harness breeching

27 Who wrote:
'Four things greater than all things are, Women and Horses, and Power and War'?
[a] Rudyard Kipling
[b] The Duke of Wellington
[c] King Charles II

28 In gambling, what is a 'nap selection'?
[a] A horse chosen with a pin
[b] The best bet of the day
[c] The horse with the least chance of winning

29 When did docking horses' tails become illegal in Britain?
[a] 1948
[b] 1955
[c] 1962

30 Who is said to have devised the lineal measurement four inches = one hand?
[a] Xenophon
[b] Leonardo da Vinci
[c] William Cavendish, Duke of Newcastle

31 What is the average capacity of the horse's small intestine?
[a] 20–30 litres
[b] 30–40 litres
[c] 40–50 litres

32 From where does the Friesian horse originate?
[a] Belgium
[b] Denmark
[c] Holland

33 Which of these trees is poisonous to horses?
[a] Ash
[b] Yew
[c] Birch

34 At what age does a horse have a full mouth of permanent teeth?
[a] Six years old
[b] Seven years old
[c] Eight years old

35 Who was the first American rider to win Badminton Horse Trials?
[a] Michael Plumb
[b] Bruce Davidson
[c] David O'Connor

36 What is a jade?
[a] An Arabian horse decoration
[b] A worn-out horse
[c] A dishonest jockey

37 What was a cock-horse?
[a] A horse used to carry poultry to market
[b] A showy horse with extravagant paces
[c] An extra horse used to help teams pull heavy loads up hills

38 The British Show Jumping High Jump record set at Olympia in 1978 still stands over 30 years later. Who was the rider?
[a] Nick Skelton
[b] Ellen Whitaker
[c] David Broome

39 Which German horse breed is marked with a traditional elk-horn brand?
[a] The Trakehner
[b] The Hanoverian
[c] The Westphalian

40 What is a chambon?
[a] A variation of the hackamore
[b] A type of gag bridle
[c] A type of schooling martingale

41 What is the digital cushion?
[a] A wedge-shaped pad filling the hollow behind a horse's heels
[b] Another name for the sensitive frog
[c] A cartilage attached to the horse's pedal bone

42 Who uses a tool called a pritchel?
[a] A loriner
[b] A saddler
[c] A farrier

43 **What does riding roughshod over someone mean?**
[a] Trampling on them
[b] Ignoring them
[c] Treating them with respect

44 **Who rides in state processions?**
[a] The master of ceremonies
[b] The Master-at-Arms
[c] The Master of the Horse

45 **What is speedy-cutting?**
[a] In racing, overtaking another horse on his inside
[b] An injury to the inside of a horse's leg caused by a blow from the opposite foot.
[c] Giving a horse a blanket clip

46 **How long is the Grand National?**
[a] About 3¾ miles
[b] About 4¼ miles
[c] About 4½ miles

47 **Where would you expect to see a ballotade?**
[a] On the polo field
[b] In high-school riding
[c] In the theatre

48 **What is the purpose of the bib on a bib martingale?**
[a] To prevent a horse catching his teeth in the straps
[b] To prevent a horse biting his neighbour
[c] To prevent a horse snatching at grass while being ridden

49 **Which pack of hounds is popularly known as the Black and Tans?**
[a] The Scarteen
[b] The Beaufort
[c] The Quorn

50 **What is a pipe-opener?**
[a] A veterinary surgeon's instrument
[b] A piece of music for a mounted band
[c] A short, sharp gallop

51 Which is the oldest
    of the British Classic
    races?
    [a] The Oaks
    [b] The St Leger
    [c] The Derby

52 What is a vaquero?
    [a] A mounted
        bullfighter
    [b] A type of lasso
    [c] A cowboy

53 Who wrote the poem
    The Old Grey Mare?
    [a] George John Whyte-
        Melville
    [b] John Masefield
    [c] John Betjeman

54 What is the term for
    three horses driven in
    single file?
    [a] Unicorn
    [b] Tandem
    [c] Random

55 Hammerhead, Box and
    Prince of Wales are all
    types of what?
    [a] Spurs
    [b] Horse-drawn vehicles
    [c] Cloth used to make
        side-saddle habits

56 Which famous actress,
    using the pseudonym
    'Mr Jersey', owned a
    string of racehorses
    and was an enthusiastic
    gambler?
    [a] Ellen Terry
    [b] Sarah Bernhardt
    [c] Lillie Langtry

57 What is the official
    world long jump record
    achieved by a horse?
    [a] 7.80 m (25 ft 7 in)
    [b] 8.10 m (25 ft 6⅞ in)
    [c] 8.40 m (27 ft 6¾ in)

58 In which of these
    English Classic races are
    fillies, as well as colts,
    allowed to compete?
    [a] The 2,000 Guineas
    [b] The Derby
    [c] The St Leger

59 What is a bluff?
    [a] An eye-cover used
        on the heads of
        excitable horses to
        keep them quiet
    [b] A misleading
        manoeuvre on the
        polo field
    [c] A type of cross-
        country drop fence

60 What is the most suitable type of shoe for a horse with collapsed heels?
[a] Half-bar
[b] Egg-bar
[c] Heart-bar

61 Where did Aimé Tschiffely travel on his famous two-and-a-half-year ride?
[a] From Cape Town to Cairo
[b] From Paris to Istanbul
[c] From Buenos Aires to Washington D.C.

62 Where is Le Musée Vivant du Cheval (the Museum of the Living Horse)?
[a] Lausanne
[b] Chantilly
[c] Brussels

63 Which tribe of North American Indians developed the Appaloosa breed?
[a] The Nez Percé
[b] The Blackfoot
[c] The Sioux

64 With which British breed of pony was Sylvia Calmady-Hamlyn associated?
[a] The Dartmoor
[b] The Exmoor
[c] The New Forest

65 What is ambling?
[a] Wandering about
[b] Stuttering
[c] Trotting irregularly

66 In which Shakespearean play does the king give the order to 'Saddle White Surrey for the field tomorrow'?
[a] *Richard II*
[b] *Richard III*
[c] *Henry V*

67 Which horse-drawn vehicle is often referred to as a 'bike'?
[a] A racing sulky
[b] A marathon cart
[c] A Governess cart

68 What out hunting is a rasper?
[a] A very big fence
[b] A horse with a cough
[c] A disobedient hound

69 In American flat racing which races make up the Triple Crown?
    [a] The Kentucky Derby, Preakness Stakes and Belmont Stakes
    [b] The Kentucky Derby, Belmont Stakes and Breeders' Cup Turf
    [c] The Kentucky Derby, Washington International and Arlington Million

70 Which famous English sporting writer used the nom de plume 'The Druid'?
    [a] Peter O'Sullivan
    [b] H.H. Dixon
    [c] R.S. Surtees

71 Where would you find the obstacle known as Pulvermann's Grave?
    [a] The Grand Pardubice Steeplechase course
    [b] The Kentucky Three-Day cross-country course
    [c] The Hamburg Jumping Derby course

72 In racing, what is an apprentice allowance?
    [a] A trainee jockey's wages
    [b] A reduction in the weight carried by a horse ridden by an apprentice
    [c] A percentage of the prize money awarded to a trainee jockey

73 When did A.J. Hansom design his two-wheeled vehicle known as the Hansom cab?
    [a] 1634
    [b] 1734
    [c] 1834

74 What is a cabriolet?
    [a] A type of bit
    [b] An advanced dressage movement
    [c] A two-wheeled horse-drawn carriage

75 How many cavalrymen were in the Charge of the Light Brigade?
    [a] 150
    [b] 600
    [c] 1,000

76 The herb elecampane used to be known as 'horse-heal' because it was believed to be a cure for which equine condition?
[a] Mange
[b] Strangles
[c] Ring-worm

77 What is/was a whirlicote?
[a] A type of mechanical horse walker
[b] A type of early conveyance used by women
[c] A type of equine coat marking

78 Which 19th-century British poet wrote: 'What do we, as a nation, care about books? How much do you think we spend altogether on our libraries, public or private, as compared with what we spend on our horses?'
[a] John Ruskin
[b] Matthew Arnold
[c] Robert Browning

79 According to folklore, a ride on a piebald horse cures a child of which illness?
[a] Measles
[b] Whooping cough
[c] Chickenpox

80 In the Chinese 12-year calendar, which is the Year of the Horse?
[a] The first year
[b] The fifth year
[c] The seventh year

81 What is a Norton Perfection?
[a] A type of bridle
[b] A type of four-wheeled horsedrawn carriage
[c] A type of trotting horse

82 Where would you find hammercloth?
[a] Covering the frame of a coachman's seat
[b] Covering a farrier's knees
[c] Covering a veterinary surgeon's operating table

83 In the ancient Roman sport of chariot racing, what was a biga?
[a] A two-horse race
[b] A two-horse chariot
[c] A signal denoting the end of the second lap

84 Every horse of which British breed can trace its descent from the stallion called Thomas Crisp's Horse of Ufford?
[a] The Suffolk
[b] The Cleveland Bay
[c] The Shire

85 Which stud farm, founded by the Emperor Joseph II, is home to the Shagya Arabian horse?
[a] Lipica
[b] Babolna
[c] Warendorf

86 What is Bellfounder?
[a] The name of a famous trotting horse
[b] A type of equine palsy
[c] An old name for a farrier

87 In a book by which English novelist did a character say, 'Those who've got horses to sell must lie'?
[a] Jane Austin
[b] Anthony Trollope
[c] Charles Dickens

88 Which famous equestrian artist learned to race-ride?
[a] George Stubbs
[b] Sir Alfred Munnings
[c] John Skeaping

89 Which famous painter of racing scenes blinded himself in one eye while lifting a dog over a hedge?
[a] George Stubbs
[b] Edgar Degas
[c] Sir Alfred Munnings

90 Which classical riding master wrote the equestrian best seller *Gli Ordini di Cavalcare* (*The Rules of Riding*)?
[a] Federico Grisone
[b] The Duke of Newcastle
[c] François Robichon de la Guérinière

91 At which English monarch's coronation did Lord Talbot's horse, on which he was required to ride into Westminster Hall to swear his allegiance, insist on approaching the throne rump first?
[a] Queen Elizabeth I's
[b] King George III's
[c] Queen Victoria's

92 Bentinck, Mameluke and Turkish are all types of what?
[a] Extinct horse breeds
[b] Bits
[c] Driving harness

93 Which famous steeple-chase is run over timber fences?
[a] The Grand Steeplechase de Paris
[b] The Maryland Hunt Cup
[c] The Pardubice

94 In which sport did the American horse Greyhound excel?
[a] Harness racing
[b] Flat racing
[c] Steeplechasing

95 Who was known as the Napoleon of the Turf?
[a] Lord Derby
[b] Lord George Bentinck
[c] King George V

96 Which sporting artist also wrote sporting articles, using the pseudonym 'Ben Tally-Ho'?
[a] Henry Alken, Senior
[b] Cecil Aldin
[c] George Denholm Armour

97 The Prix de Diane is the French equivalent of which British race?
[a] The Cheltenham Gold Cup
[b] The Oaks
[c] The Princess of Wales's Stakes

98 Spider, skeleton and whiskey are types of what?
[a] Harness
[b] Foxhounds
[c] Gigs (two-wheeled, horse-drawn vehicles)

99 Of which modern
horse breed was the
Middle Ages packhorse
known as the Chapman
Horse said to be the
foundation?
[a] The Hackney
[b] The Cleveland Bay
[c] The Clydesdale

100 Which British poet was
the son of a livery-
stable keeper?
[a] John Keats
[b] William Wordsworth
[c] Lord Byron

?

Who's
Who?

101 Who makes bits?
[a] A saddler
[b] A loriner
[c] A cooper

102 Whose walls are jumped at Badminton?
[a] Tom Smith's
[b] Bill Smith's
[c] Jack Smith's

103 Who uses an anvil?
[a] A veterinary surgeon
[b] A farrier
[c] A horse dentist

104 Which jockey won the Grand National in 2010 on his fifteenth attempt?
[a] Tony Dobbin
[b] Ruby Walsh
[c] A.P. McCoy

105 Who perform flags, arabesques and prince seats?
[a] Western riders
[b] Vaulters
[c] High school riders

106 Who is the patron saint of huntsmen?
[a] St Hubert
[b] St Cuthbert
[c] St Christopher

107 Which empress caused a sensation when she visited England and hunted with the Pytchley hounds?
[a] Maria Theresa
[b] Catherine the Great
[c] Elizabeth of Austria

108 Who wrote the book *My Dancing White Horses*?
[a] Hans Handler
[b] Alois Podhajsky
[c] The Duke of Newcastle

109 Who won Badminton in 2010?
[a] Paul Tapner on Inonothing
[b] Mark Todd on Grass Valley
[c] William Fox-Pitt on Macchiato

110 Who in legend is said to have created the horse?
[a] Hector
[b] Neptune
[c] Achilles

111 Who rode Cortaflex Mondriaan to victory in the British Jumping Derby at Hickstead in 2006, 2008 and 2009?
[a] Michael Whitaker
[b] William Funnell
[c] Pippa Funnell

112 Who is the Patron of the Cleveland Bay Horse Society?
[a] HM The Queen
[b] HRH The Princess Royal
[c] HRH The Prince of Wales

113 Which R.S. Surtees character advises riders, when jumping, to 'throw your heart over and then follow it as quickly as you can'?
[a] Mr Jorrocks
[b] Mr Sponge
[c] Lucy Glitters

114 Who wrote Right Royal, the epic steeplechasing poem?
[a] John Masefield
[b] John Betjeman
[c] John Keats

115 Which child actress, who went on to success as an adult, starred in the 1944 film National Velvet and was made a Dame in 1999?
[a] Julie Andrews
[b] Elizabeth Taylor
[c] Joan Collins

116 Who uses an endoscope?
[a] A veterinary surgeon
[b] A wheelwright
[b] A show jumping course builder

117 Out hunting, who should wear loose ribbon tails on their caps?
[a] All mounted followers
[b] All mounted followers over the age of 18
[c] Only hunt servants and officials

118 Who uses a lariat?
[a] A vaulter
[b] A cowboy
[c] A mounted bullfighter

119 Who was Sir Edwin Landseer?
 [a] The most famous animal painter of his day
 [b] The most famous veterinary surgeon of his day
 [c] The most famous breeder of racehorses of his day

120 Who wears a hat with a veil, a habit and one spur?
 [a] A circus rider
 [b] A side-saddle rider
 [c] A female Western rider

121 Who controls the followers of a hunt when hounds are drawing or hunting?
 [a] The whipper-in
 [b] The master
 [c] The field master

122 Who drives a horse from the saddle, riding the nearside horse?
 [a] A groom
 [b] A postillion
 [c] An outrider

123 Who makes carriage wheels and puts on the tyres?
 [a] A cartwright
 [b] A wainwright
 [c] A wheelwright

124 Who foolishly accepted the gift of a huge wooden horse?
 [a] The Greeks
 [b] The Romans
 [c] The Trojans

125 Who broke the freestyle dressage world record twice in 2009?
 [a] Edward Gal on Moorlands Totilas
 [b] Laura Bechtolsheimer on Mistral Hojris
 [c] Anky van Grunsven on Salinero

126 Who might find themselves in the horse latitudes?
[a] Becalmed sailors
[b] Endurance riders
[c] Mexican cowboys

127 Who raise their hats to the Emperor Karl VI?
[a] The riders of the Spanish Riding School of Vienna
[b] The riders of the Cadre Noir
[c] Portuguese mounted bullfighters

128 Who invented the early form of horseshoe known as the hipposandal?
[a] The Phoenicians
[b] The Greeks
[c] The Romans

129 Who won gold in the individual three-day event at the 2008 Beijing Olympics?
[a] Hinrich Romeike on Marius
[b] Mark Todd on Gandalf
[c] Mary King on Call Again Cavalier

130 Who was the first woman jockey to complete the Grand National course?
[a] Elaine Mellor
[b] Geraldine Rees
[c] Lorna Vincent

131 Which member of the British Royal Family won the Droitwich Chase at Worcester on Cnoc na Cuille?
[a] HRH The Prince of Wales
[b] HRH Prince Edward
[c] HRH The Princess Royal

132 Which Australian event rider won a team gold medal at the 1992, 1996 and 2000 Olympics?
[a] Stuart Tinney
[b] Andrew Hoy
[c] Matt Ryan

133 Who won the FEI World Cup Show Jumping Final in 2008 and 2009?
[a] Meredith Michaels-Beerbaum
[b] Ludger Beerbaum
[c] Marcus Ehning

134 Who is Victoria Grace?
   [a] A leading British polo player
   [b] A leading British side-saddle rider
   [c] A leading British vaulter

135 Who founded a hospital for old war horses in Cairo?
   [a] Dorothy Brooke
   [b] Glenda Spooner
   [c] Ada Cole

136 Who were the first horse and rider to win the Burghley three-day event?
   [a] Merely-A-Monarch and Anneli Drummond-Hay
   [b] High And Mighty and Sheila Willcox
   [c] Be Fair and Lucinda Prior-Palmer

137 In 2008, who was the Canadian rider who won, in their ninth Olympic Games, their first Olympic medal?
   [a] Ian Millar
   [b] Jill Henselwood
   [c] Eric Lamaze

138 Who uses a tool called a searcher?
   [a] A farrier
   [b] A veterinary surgeon
   [c] An equine dentist

139 Which rider missed qualification for the 2008 Olympic Games due to a leg infection in her horse, Locarno 62?
   [a] Ben Maher
   [b] Ellen Whitaker
   [c] Tina Fletcher

140 Who rides on the 'horse with ten toes'?
   [a] A high school rider
   [b] A walker
   [c] A gambler

141 Who was the first woman to win an Olympic medal for show jumping?
   [a] Marion Mould
   [b] Liz Edgar
   [c] Pat Smythe

142 Who rode Shergar when he won the Epsom Derby?
   [a] Lester Piggott
   [b] Walter Swinburn
   [c] Willie Carson

143 Which mounted messenger was known as the courier of the American Revolution and was immortalised in a poem by Longfellow?
[a] Paul Revere
[b] William 'Buffalo Bill' Cody
[c] George Washington

144 Which Russian aristocrat founded a famous breed of trotting horse?
[a] Count Alexis Orlov
[b] Prince Felix Youssoupoff
[c] Prince Nicolas Borissovitch

145 Which German Olympic show jumper became a harness racing trainer?
[a] Paul Schockemöhle
[b] Alwin Schockemöhle
[c] Hans Günter Winkler

146 Who rode a horse called Ruksh?
[a] Rob Roy
[b] Robin Hood
[c] Rustum

147 Who was Nuno Oliveira?
[a] A 19th-century Portuguese mounted bullfighter
[b] A 1950s Portuguese show jumper
[c] A 20th-century Portuguese riding master

148 In Greek mythology, who destroyed himself by attempting to drive the horses of his father, the sun god Helios?
[a] Peleus
[b] Phaeton
[c] Pollux

149 For her illustrations for which book was Lucy Kemp-Welch particularly well -known?
[a] *Moorland Mousie*
[b] *Black Beauty*
[c] *Handley Cross*

150 Who rode half of the Badminton three-day event course with only one stirrup?
[a] Mark Todd
[b] Andrew Nicholson
[c] Ian Stark

151 St Eloi is the patron saint of whom?
[a] Blacksmiths
[b] Saddlers
[c] Veterinary surgeons

152 Newmarket racecourse is said to be haunted by the ghost of which jockey, who shot himself at the age of 29?
[a] Jack Watts
[b] Samuel Chifney
[c] Fred Archer

153 Which show jumping brothers made history by winning gold and silver medals at the same Olympic Games?
[a] Michael and John Whitaker
[b] Paul and Alwin Schockemöhle
[c] Raimondo and Piero d'Inzeo

154 Who was known as 'the father of classical equitation'?
[a] Federico Caprilli
[b] François Robichon de la Guérinière
[c] Xenophon

155 Which monarch's statue, on horseback and with sword raised aloft, stands in Old Palace Yard, Westminster?
[a] Richard the Third
[b] Richard the Lionheart
[c] Edward I

156 The hero of which Shakespearean comedy complains 'What, no man at door to hold my stirrup nor to take my horse'?
[a] Bassanio in The Merchant of Venice
[b] Berown in Love's Labour's Lost
[c] Petruchio in The Taming of the Shrew

157 Which writer in his Dictionary of the English Language described oats as 'a grain which in England is generally given to horses, but in Scotland supports the people'?
[a] Charles Dickens
[b] Dr Samuel Johnson
[c] Anthony Trollope

158 Who wrote: 'For myself, I should prefer three falls astride to one sideways, and I have had considerable experience of both'?
[a] Muriel Wace, known as 'Golden Gorse', author of *Moorland Mousie*
[b] Robert Smith Surtees, creator of the famous sporting character John Jorrocks
[c] Anna Sewell, author of *Black Beauty*

159 Which German world champion show jumper died at the age of 36 following a car crash?
[a] Hartwig Steenken
[b] Hendrik Snoek
[c] Fritz Thiedemann

160 Who wrote: 'The one best rule and practice in dealing with horses is never to lose your temper'?
[a] Xenophon
[b] R.S. Surtees
[c] R.S. Summerhays

161 Which Irish dramatist wrote: 'Go anywhere in England where there are natural, wholesome, contented and really nice English people and what do you find?
That the stables are the real centre of the household'?
[a] Oscar Wilde
[b] William Butler Yeats
[c] George Bernard Shaw

162 Who followed Infanta Pilar, Duchess of Badajoz, as the president of the FEI (Fédération Équestre Internationale)?
[a] HRH The Princess Royal
[b] HRH Princess Haya Bint Al Hussein
[c] HRH Prince Philip, Duke of Edinburgh

163 Who uses a creasing iron?
[a] A saddle or harness maker
[b] A farrier
[c] A bit maker

164 Who famously rode the winner of the Grand Steeplechase de Paris on a horse whose bit had broken after jumping only three fences?
[a] Fred Winter
[b] Tim Brookshaw
[c] Dick Francis

165 Which nobleman wrote the classic book, *A New Method, and Extraordinary Invention, to Dress Horses, and Work Them According to Nature...*?
[a] William Cavendish, first Duke of Newcastle
[b] Field Marshal Arthur Wellesley, first Duke of Wellington
[c] Sir Edmund of Langley, first Duke of York

166 Which English king died after falling when his horse stumbled over a mole hill?
[a] Edward III
[b] Henry III
[c] William III

167 Who wear kneepads when riding?
[a] Side-saddle riders
[b] Polo players
[c] Vaulters

168 Who wrote: 'My horses understand me tolerably well; I converse with them at least four hours every day'?
[a] Jonathan Swift
[b] Samuel Pepys
[c] Oscar Wilde

169 Who won the team silver medal in the 2001 FEI European Show Jumping Championships —their first senior jumping medal since 1932?
[a] Ireland
[b] Sweden
[c] Belgium

170 Who holds the world speed record for changing a team of horses?
[a] George Bowman, Senior
[b] John Parker
[c] George Bowman, Junior

171 Who was the eccentric horseman whose extraordinary exploits included driving his tandem across country at night?
[a] The 5th Earl of Lonsdale
[b] Sir Charles Bunbury
[c] 'Mad Jack' Mytton

172 Which sporting artist wrote a pamphlet entitled The Folly and Crime of Docking Horses over a century before the practice was banned in Britain?
[a] Lucy Kemp-Welch
[b] George Stubbs
[c] James Ward

173 Who rides The Pale Horse?
[a] Death
[b] War
[c] Peace

174 Who introduced the pillars into haute école training?
[a] The Greek General Xenophon
[b] The 17th-century riding master Antoine de Pluvinel
[c] The 20th-century director of the Spanish Riding School, Alois Podhajsky

175 Who famously went under (rather than over) an obstacle on the Badminton cross-country course—a manoeuvre which led to a rule change?
[a] Rachel Bayliss on Gurgle The Greek
[b] Captain Mark Phillips on Great Ovation
[c] Virginia Leng on Priceless

176 A newspaper ad in 1860 read: 'Wanted: young, skinny, wiry fellows not over 18. Must be expert riders willing to risk life daily. Orphans preferred.' What would the successful applicants be doing?
[a] Russian circus trick riders
[b] British cavalry recruits
[c] Pony Express riders in America

177 Who wrote: 'the seat on a horse makes gentlemen of some and grooms of others'?
[a] Miguel de Cervantes in *Don Quixote*
[b] Jane Austen in *Pride and Prejudice*
[c] William Cobbett in *Rural Rides*

178 Who wrote the racing poem *How We Beat the Favourite*?
[a] Adam Lindsay Gordon
[b] Robert Browning
[c] Will H. Ogilvie

179 Who were Gotthard and Gustave Schumann?
[a] Renowned composers who wrote music for equestrian quadrilles and carousels
[b] Renowned riders who founded the Schumann Circus specialising in equestrian acts
[c] Renowned carriage drivers of the 19th century

180 Who was Tregonwell Frampton?
[a] Racing manager to four British monarchs and known as 'The Father of Racing'
[b] A notorious 19th-century English gambler
[c] A maker of racing sulkies in America

181 Who introduced the first horsedrawn firefighting service?
[a] The Emperor Augustus
[b] Napoleon Bonaparte
[c] King Henry VIII

182 Which character in Shakespeare's *The Merchant of Venice*, who never actually appears on stage, 'doth nothing but talk of his horse'?
[a] The Count Palatine
[b] The Neapolitan Prince
[c] Falconbridge

183 Who wrote the classic foxhunting work, *Thoughts on Hunting*?
[a] Lord Willoughby de Broke
[b] Peter Beckford
[c] A. Mackay-Smith

184 Which influential figure in the history of racing is buried in Goldsborough Church in Yorkshire?
[a] Captain Robert Byerley, owner of The Byerley Turk
[b] The 12th Earl of Derby
[c] Admiral the Hon Henry John Rous

185 Who wrote a poem called *A Dialogue Between Two Horses*, in which two London statues, left alone for the evening by their royal riders, gossip and grumble about the state of the nation?
[a] John Orr Ewing
[b] Ted Hughes
[c] Andrew Marvell

186 Whose horse was El Morzillo?
[a] Christopher Columbus
[b] Vasco da Gama
[c] The Conquistador Hernán Cortés

187 Who claimed to be the only woman ever to win the chariot race at Olympia?
[a] Cynisca, sister of Agesilaus, King of Sparta
[b] Antonia, daughter of the Roman Emperor Claudius
[c] Poppaea, wife of the Roman emperor Nero

188 Who wrote, 'Hunting is the noblest exercise, makes man laborious, active wise, brings health and doth the spirits delight?'
[a] Cecil Aldin
[b] Lionel Dawson
[c] Ben Jonson

189 Which trainer trained the winner of the Grand National four times, with Amberleigh House winning once and Red Rum on three occasions?
[a] Donald 'Ginger' McCain
[b] Venetia Williams
[c] Jonjo O'Neill

190 Who rode backwards up Holborn Hill?
[a] Dick Whittington, Lord Mayor of London
[b] Witches on brooksticks
[c] Condemned prisoners on their way to be hanged at Tyburn

191 In *Auguries of Innocence*, who wrote: 'A Horse misus'd upon the Road Calls to Heaven for Human blood'?
[a] William Blake
[b] Mark Twain
[c] Charles Lamb

192 Who, in Shakespeare's play *Cymbeline*, cries 'O for a horse with wings!'?
[a] Cymbeline, King of Britain
[b] Imogen
[c] Giacomo

193 Who used a yard of tin?
[a] A wheelwright
[b] An old livery yard keeper
[c] The guard on a Royal Mail coach

194 Which queen had a favourite palfrey called Rosabelle?
[a] Isabella of Spain
[b] Marie Antoinette of France
[c] Mary Queen of Scots

195 Who fed strangers to his horses?
[a] The Thracian Diomedes
[b] The Roman Emperor Caligula
[c] The Mongol Genghis Khan

196 Who vanquished the tyrant who fed strangers to his horses and gave his carcass to them to eat?
[a] The Roman Emperor Claudius
[b] Hercules
[c] The Holy Roman Emperor Frederick Barbarossa

197 In Wagner's opera *Götterdämmerung* (*The Twilight of the Gods*) who rides her horse Grane into Siegfried's funeral pyre?
[a] Flosshilde
[b] Sieglinde
[c] Brünnhilde

198 Horsepower equals the power required to raise 3,000 lb by 1 ft (14,982 kg by 30.48 cm) per minute. Who set this measurement?
[a] Isambard Kingdom Brunel
[b] James Watt
[c] George Stephenson

199 Who was the Army vet, also a sculptor, whose works include the quadriga on top of the arch at Hyde Park Corner in London?
[a] Adrian Smith
[b] Adrian Jones
[c] Adrian Hughes

200 Which 3rd-century bishop, writer and martyr was also a noted horse doctor?
[a] St Hippolytus
[b] St Boniface
[c] St Stephen of Hungary

201 What name describes a horse that is half-Thoroughbred, half-Arabian?
[a] Anglo-Arab
[b] Half-bred
[c] Arab-cross

202 According to Shakespeare, at the Battle of Bosworth Field what did Richard III offer in exchange for a horse?
[a] His palace
[b] His brother
[c] His kingdom

203 In show jumping and eventing, what colour flag marks the right-hand extremity of a fence?
[a] Red
[b] White
[c] Blue

204 What was the new name adopted by the British governing body for eventing in 2001?
[a] British Horse Trials Association
[b] British Eventing
[c] Horse Trials Society of Great Britain

205 What is a Barker brougham a type of?
[a] A foxhound
[b] A horsedrawn carriage
[c] A cross-country obstacle

206 What is another name for a Scorrier snaffle?
[a] Gag snaffle
[b] Magenis snaffle
[c] Cornish snaffle

207 What is a leaping head?
[a] The pommel on a side-saddle that curves outwards over the rider's thigh
[b] A big bank jumped when hunting in Ireland
[c] A particularly lively bull in a rodeo

208 In polocrosse, what is a face-off?
[a] Another name for riding off
[b] The start of the game when the umpire throws in the ball
[c] A penalty shot

209 What is a cinch?
[a] A western girth
[b] A hot favourite in a race
[c] A safety brake device used by carriage drivers

210 What is a Kimblewick?
[a] A type of girth
[b] A type of bit
[c] A type of fence jumped when hunting in Leicestershire

211 In America, what is an in-hand class called?
[a] Halter class
[b] Bridle class
[c] Lead class

212 What are grass tips?
[a] Shortened shoes designed to protect the toes of a horse out at grass?
[b] Chopped fresh grass used to mix in a horse's feed to stimulate his appetite
[c] Information about the chances of racehorses given to gamblers by stable employees

213 What sort of drug is phenylbutazone?
[a] An antibiotic
[b] A sedative
[c] A painkiller

214 What are wheelers?
[a] In carriage driving, horses nearest to the vehicle
[b] Dishonest horse dealers
[c] Horses who shy at the slightest things

215 What do Aunt Sally, Chase Me Charlie and Moat and Castle have in common?
[a] They are all varieties of show jumping competitions
[b] They are all varieties of mounted game
[c] They are all varieties of hunter trials

216 What is an anvil?
[a] An iron base used for shaping horseshoes
[b] A hunting horn
[c] A kick-over bolt fitted to the bottom of a stable door

217 What is a sarcoid?
   [a] A bony enlargement
      of the hock
   [b] A tumour on the skin
   [c] A crack in the hoof
      wall

218 A mule is the offspring
   of which of the
   following combinations?
   [a] Male donkey /
      Female horse
   [b] Male horse / Female
      donkey
   [c] Male ass / Female
      horse

219 What is alfalfa?
   [a] Decorative harness
      worn by Arabian
      horses in Egypt
   [b] A type of all-weather
      riding surface
   [c] A variety of lucerne
      grown as a fodder
      crop

220 What did international
   show jumper Nick
   Skelton do in the year
   2000 which caused him
   to retire?
   [a] Broke his back
   [b] Broke his neck
   [c] Fractured his skull

221 What is a lariat?
   [a] A Western girth
   [b] A lasso
   [c] An American bit
      maker

222 What material, when
   incorporated in
   horseshoes, helps to
   prevent horses slipping?
   [a] Tungsten carbide
   [b] Aluminium
   [c] Steel

223 What is a horse-
   wrangler?
   [a] An equine dentist
   [b] A writer of horsey
      fiction
   [c] A breaker-in or
      herder of horses

224 In medieval times, what
   was a destrier?
   [a] Horse armour
   [b] A knight's warhorse
   [c] A jousting lance

225 What, poetically speaking,
   are white horses?
   [a] Fast-moving clouds
   [b] White-capped
      breakers rolling in
      from the sea
   [c] Pleasant dreams

226 **Out hunting, what is a second horseman?**
[a] A joint-master
[b] An assistant field master
[c] Someone who follows the hunt quietly on a rider's second horse until the fresh horse is needed

227 **What is tic-tac?**
[a] A closely-fought finish where first one horse is in front, then another
[b] Sign language used by bookmakers to communicate with each other
[c] The noise made when horses brush through the tops of steeplechase fences

228 **What do Captain Martin William Becher and the racehorse Valentine have in common?**
[a] Both won the Grand National
[b] Both have Grand National fences named after them
[c] Both were killed while competing in the Grand National

229 **In Scotland, what is the Grey Mare's Tail?**
[a] A twisting highland road
[b] A waterfall
[c] A lengthy and highly unlikely story

230 **What is a Knabstrup?**
[a] A breed of spotted horse from Denmark
[b] A safety device specially designed to stop carriages turning over
[c] A stolen horse

231 **In classical equitation, what is often referred to as 'the black mass'?**
[a] A herd of young Lipizzaner horses whose coats have not yet turned grey
[b] The teachings of Federico Caprilli
[c] The quadrille performed by the Cadre Noir

232 Under international rules, what piece of equipment may show jumping horses not wear?
[a] A running martingale
[b] A standing martingale
[c] A dropped noseband

233 What is the meaning of the Latin phrase *caveat emptor*, often quoted when someone is buying a horse?
[a] Never trust a horse dealer
[b] Don't go away empty-handed
[c] Let the buyer beware

234 What are tugs?
[a] Horses hitched to teams to pull heavy loads
[b] Leather bands through which the shafts of a vehicle pass to prevent it tipping up or down
[c] Large studs fitted to draught horses' shoes in wet weather

235 What is an Australian cheeker?
[a] A horse used for herding cattle
[b] A type of noseband made of rubber
[c] Blinkers designed to restrict the vision of a harness horse

236 In racing, what is a maiden?
[a] A woman jockey
[b] A two-year-old filly
[c] A horse which has yet to win a race

237 What sort of gait is the tack?
[a] A fast trot
[b] A lateral gait similar to the pace
[c] A fast, elevated four-beat gait

238 What is a Toptani?
[a] A breed of Pony found in mountainous regions of Chile
[b] A jumping saddle
[c] A hat formerly worn by women riding side-saddle

239 What significant book was first published in 1791?
[a] An English translation of the works of Xenophon
[b] Volume one of *The General Stud Book*
[c] *Breaking and Training* by James Fillis

240 What is a keratoma?
[a] A circus horse used by acrobats
[b] A type of horse found in southern Russia
[c] A horny tumour on the inner surfaces of the wall of a horse's foot

241 What is a stringhalt?
[a] A now-illegal method of tripping up galloping horses during filmmaking
[b] An involuntary snatching up of the hind legs when a horse is walking
[c] A primitive method of restraining horses during surgical procedures

242 What is a Peruvian Paso?
[a] A breed of horse with distinctive four-beat gaits
[b] An illegal manoeuvre in polo
[c] A gymkhana game

243 What is the 'fox trot', as demonstrated by the Missouri Fox Trotting Horse?
[a] An elevated trot similar to the passage
[b] A four-beat running gait
[c] A smooth gait in which the horse walks with its forelegs and trots behind

244 What are heel extensions?
[a] Very long spurs
[b] Surgical horseshoes that are extended backwards beyond the hoof
[c] Extra-long shafts on carriages to prevent a horse that kicks from damaging himself or the vehicle

245 Apron and bib are types of what?
[a] Clip
[b] Side-saddle habit
[c] Waterproof rug

246 What is the English equivalent of the French term *l'épaule en dedans*?
[a] Shoulder-in
[b] Shoulder-out
[c] Turn on the forehand

247 What name is given to a herdsman of the Camargue, in France?
[a] Conservateur
[b] Gardian
[c] Garde-chasse

248 For what is the Thoroughbred horse Grakle, after whom a noseband was named, famous?
[a] He won the Grand National in 1931
[b] He was the favourite hunter of King George V
[c] He is the subject of a painting by George Stubbs

249 What does the word hippopotamus mean?
[a] Like a horse
[b] Horse of the river
[c] African horse

250 What brought to an end the brilliant Mill Reef's flat-racing career?
[a] A complicated fracture of his near foreleg
[b] Respiratory disease
[c] Twisted gut

251 In what business did Richard Tattersall make his name?
[a] Horse sales
[b] Horse transport
[c] Horse training

252 In racing, what colour flag is used to indicate a false start?
[a] Blue
[b] Red
[c] Yellow

253 What sort of microorganism causes the disease strangles?
[a] A virus
[b] A fungus
[c] A bacterium

254 In July 2001, Quixall Crosseth set which record?
[a] He became the oldest horse ever to take part in a British horse race
[b] He refused to leave the stalls for the twentieth time
[c] He became the only horse in Britain to race a hundred times and never win

255 Under FEI rules, what is the maximum height of a show jumping obstacle in a Grand Prix-level competition?
[a] 2 m (6.5 ft)
[b] 2.25 m (7.38 ft)
[c] 1.5 m (4.92 ft)

256 What did George Shillibeer introduce into London, from Paris, in 1829?
[a] The horse-drawn omnibus
[b] The docking of horse's tails
[c] The bearing rein

257 What flower is used in the brand-mark of Austria's Haflinger pony?
[a] Edelweiss
[b] Orchid
[c] Poppy

258 What is the meaning of the Mexican Spanish word *mesteno*, from which the term Mustang comes?
[a] Foreigner
[b] Nomad
[c] A stray animal

259 **What is a blood weed?**
[a] A lightly-built Thoroughbred horse lacking bone and substance
[b] A highly poisonous plant
[c] A type of leech

260 **What is an ekka?**
[a] A one-horse cart used in India
[b] A type of horse found in Iceland
[c] A horse who lacks the ability to neigh

261 **One of Ireland's racecourses is called The Curragh. What does Curragh mean?**
[a] Course for horse
[b] Swift horse
[c] Meeting place

262 **In the USA, what is a Welara?**
[a] A manoeuvre performed in the sport of running
[b] A Welsh/Arab cross
[c] A type of waterproof riding boot

263 **What is an 'iron horse'?**
[a] A dark grey horse
[b] A steam locomotive
[c] A horse who is never lame

264 **What is a Bashkir Curly?**
[a] A thick rug used by troika drivers
[b] A hardy breed of horse originating in Russia
[c] A reindeer skin saddle cover used by Mongolian herdsmen

265 **What is the weight of a polo ball?**
[a] 120–135 g (4.5–4.75 oz)
[b] 142–170 g (5–6 oz)
[c] 184–198 g (6.5–7 oz)

266 **What is a back jockey?**
[a] Part of a Western saddle
[b] A rider who leans back in the saddle with his feet sticking forwards
[c] A race rider who deliberately stops a horse winning a race

267 In England, what is the traditional badge of the county of Kent?
[a] A white horse
[b] A black horse
[c] A bay horse

268 Hengist and Horsa were said to have led the first Saxon invasion of England. What does the word hengist mean?
[a] Warhorse
[b] Stallion
[c] Conqueror

269 What is a reata?
[a] A Mexican lariat or lasso
[b] A horse fair in Ecuador
[c] An evasive movement used in mounted bullfighting

270 What is the more familiar name for a 'turn-row' horse?
[a] Morgan Horse
[b] Tennessee Walking Horse
[c] Missouri Fox Trotting Horse

271 What are hame terretts?
[a] Highland ponies with a well-developed homing instinct
[b] Rings on a horse's harness through which the reins pass
[c] Safety fastenings for the cups on show jumping supports

272 What is a buttero?
[a] A horse used in mounted bullfighting
[b] A Spanish safety stirrup
[c] An Italian mounted herdsman

273 What did the Englishwoman Norah Wilmot do even though it was not officially permitted for women until 1966?
[a] Rode in steeplechases
[b] Competed in show jumping Nations Cup teams
[c] Trained racehorses

274 **What is or was a planchette?**

[a] A water obstacle on a French cross-country course

[b] A wooden board on an old type of saddle designed for women to rest their feet

[c] A high school movement in which the horse jumps over an imaginary obstacle

275 **What type of equipment bore the names McLellan, Markham and Nolan's?**

[a] Cavalry saddles

[b] Cavalry bridles

[c] Cavalry bits

276 In the United States what name is given to a Morgan horse crossed with an Arabian?
[a] Morab
[b] Aragan
[c] Morgarab

277 What does 'to ride bodkin' mean?
[a] To travel in a carriage squeezed in between two other people
[b] To ride without a saddle or bridle
[c] To ride pillion on a horse

278 What was founded in 1921?
[a] International Olympic Committee
[b] Aachen Horse Show
[c] Fédération Équestre Internationale (FEI)

279 Where were the 2009 FEI European Show Jumping Championships held?
[a] Aachen
[b] Hickstead
[c] Windsor

280 What is the meaning of the expression 'to fig up a horse'?
[a] To groom it thoroughly for a special occasion
[b] To increase its height by fitting thick shoes
[c] To make it more lively by artificial means

281 In driving, what are known as thrills?
[a] Reins
[b] Shafts
[c] Traces

282 What is the meaning of the Balti word *pulu* from which the name polo derives?
[a] Polo
[b] Goal
[c] Ball

283 What is a Mangalarga Marchador?
[a] A type of severe curb bit
[b] A breed of horse found in Brazil
[c] An Argentinean cattle rancher

284 What did the American Horse Shows Association change its name to in 2001?
[a] United States Equestrian Society
[b] United States Horse Shows Association
[c] USA Equestrian

285 What did the American James Todhunter Sloan introduce into Britain in 1897?
[a] The Standardbred harness racehorse
[b] The crouching style of flat-race riding
[c] The Western saddle

286 What in the 18th century did Philip Astley discover?
[a] The last remaining wild horses in America
[b] That by cantering a horse around a 13-metre diameter circle a rider could balance on its croup by virtue of centrifugal force
[c] A skeleton of eohippus

287 Bucephalus was the horse that carried Alexander the Great through his Asia campaigns. What does the word bucephalus mean?
[a] Big horse
[b] Warrior
[c] Ox face

288 What is or was The Tantivy Trot?
[a] An uneven trot indicating lameness in a horse
[b] A popular 19th-century coaching song
[c] Another name for the rising trot

289 What are futchells?
[a] Fastenings which secure the splinter bar to the axle-tree on a coach
[b] Biting insects which spread African horse sickness
[c] Tendon boots specially designed for polo ponies

290 In Chaucer's *Squire's Tale*, what was remarkable about the Brazen Horse given by the King of Arabia and India to Cambuscan, King of Sarra?
[a] It could speak five languages
[b] By giving it instructions and turning a pin in its ear it would carry its rider anywhere
[c] It could foretell the future

291 What did newspaper tycoon James Gordon Bennett Junior introduce into America in 1878?
[a] The game of polo
[b] Shire horses
[c] The first magazine for horse owners

292 What was a two-legged mare?
[a] A broken-down old horse
[b] The gallows
[c] A horse with a habit of rearing

293 What is a donga?
[a] An horse-drawn taxi
[b] The arch which passes over a horse's neck in typical Russian harness
[c] A steady old mare who wears a bell around her neck so that the rest of the herd will follow her

294 In America in 1860, what did William H. Russell found?
[a] The National Horse Show in New York
[b] The world's first harness racecourse
[c] The Pony Express mail service

295 In horse conformation, what is referred to as the 'jibbah'?
[a] The angle at which a horse's head joins its neck
[b] The shield-shaped bulge on the head of an Arabian horse
[c] The space between a horse's front legs

296 What is a shadow roll?
  [a] A type of blinker worn by carriage horses
  [b] A groom's seat on a mail coach
  [c] An attachment to a harness racing bridle to prevent a horse spooking at shadows on the ground

297 What is or was a 'flying trench'?
  [a] A type of thin bit, the forerunner of the bridoon
  [b] A school or air above the ground
  [c] An early type of eventing obstacle consisting of a fence over a small ditch

298 In driving, what is a Manchester team?
  [a] A unicorn
  [b] A trandem
  [c] A team of four

299 In racing, what is a conditions race?
  [a] A non-handicap
  [b] An apprentice race
  [c] A race for amateur jockeys

300 What is or was an 'upper Benjamin'?
  [a] A member of the arena party at a horse show
  [b] An overcoat worn by coachmen
  [c] A room for a groom, situated above the stables

? True or False?

301 The Pony Club is the largest association of young riders in the world.

302 Ragwort is highly poisonous to horses.

303 All Lipizzaner horses are born grey.

304 Women riders were barred from the Olympic three-day event until 1964.

305 Horses should never be watered before being fed.

306 It is virtually impossible for horses to vomit.

307 If a horse has pigeon toes, his front feet turn outwards.

308 For safety, a rider's tiepin should never be worn vertically.

309 The average girth measurement of a Shire horse stallion is 180–240 cm (or 6–8 ft).

310 The Duke of Edinburgh drove a team of Highland ponies owned by HM The Queen.

311 Red Rum is the only horse to have won the Grand National three times.

312 A Table C is a show jumping competition with one jump-off against the clock.

313 Horses do not suffer from worms when they are over 20-years-old.

314 Linseed should always be cooked before being fed to horses.

315 Navicular is a type of equine respiratory disease.

316 Horses are able to sleep standing up.

317 Burmese was a favourite mare of HM The Queen, ridden at the ceremony of Trooping the Colour.

318 The Spanish walk is a movement performed by the horses of the Spanish Riding School of Vienna.

319 A Hobday operation is a procedure which relieves obstruction of a horse's air passage.

320 There is no such thing as an albino or pure white horse.

321 In eventing, there is no steeplechase in a CIC competition.

322 There is no Pony Club in New Zealand.

323 Carriage driving is one of the Olympic Games' equestrian sports.

324 In the USA, Virginia is known as the 'Blue Grass State'.

325 A thoroughpin is inflammation of the fetlock joint.

326 A hinny is the offspring of a male horse and a female ass.

327 The last round of the 2010 Meydan FEI Nations Cup, where the French were crowned champions for the second successive year, was held in Dublin.

328 A harness racehorse can trot or pace at a speed of some 25mph.

329 In international dressage competitions riders are allowed to carry a whip.

330 William the Conqueror died as the result of a riding accident.

331 Arabian horses have fewer ribs than other breeds.

332 Gamgee tissue was invented by Joseph Sampson Gamgee— who was both a doctor and a veterinary surgeon.

333 In olden times riding whips were often made of rowan wood which was believed to protect horses from witches' spells.

334 The Melbourne Cup is a famous polo tournament.

335 Admiral Lord Nelson had a horseshoe nailed to the mast of his flagship HMS *Victory*.

336 The English riding master James Fillis taught his horses to canter backwards.

337 No mare has ever won an individual show jumping gold medal at the Olympic Games.

338 Monday morning disease is another name for azoturia or 'tying up'.

339 Great Britain is the only country in the world to stage three-day events at four-star level.

340 In the United States a dun-coloured horse is called a buckskin.

341 The horse has no collarbone.

342 A barrage is a type of show jumping fence.

343 In Australia and New Zealand all Thoroughbred horses have their official birthday on August 1.

344 In Western riding the basic gaits are the walk, the jog and the lope.

345 Meredith Michaels-Beerbaum is married to Ludger Beerbaum.

346 A long, curly, shaggy coat is one of the symptoms of Cushing's disease.

347 Horses cannot be infected by the salmonella family of bacteria.

348 Horsing stone is another name for a mounting block.

349 Galvayne's groove is a mark found on a horse's corner incisor teeth from the age of about nine.

350 St Christopher is the patron saint of all horsemen.

351 In the sport of harness racing horses are always driven, never ridden.

352 The word *cavalletti* means small horses or trestles.

353 Horses in high jump competitions are allowed two attempts at each height.

354 The length of a horse's small intestine is about the same as the width of a dressage arena.

355 A rumble is a seat for two grooms on a private or road coach.

356 Nijinsky, ridden by Lester Piggott, was the only horse to win the English Triple Crown (the 2,000 Guineas, the Derby and the St Leger) in the second half of the 20th century.

357 Lymphangitis is an infection of the horse's throat and neck.

358 A Karrozin is a breed of horse in Malta.

359 The plant equisetum, commonly known as mare's tail or horse tail, has the same toxic effect on horses as bracken.

360 In 1929 a jockey with an artificial leg rode the winner of the Irish Grand National.

361 Fununculosis is a bacterial infection of the skin caused by infected hair follicles.

362 A Britzscha was a popular 19th-century travelling carriage designed to allow passengers to lie full length on long journeys.

363 A fiddle is a square harness buckle.

364 The Celts believed that after their death their souls were carried on horseback to the land of the dead.

365 A kelpie is a water sprite or demon that usually appears in the shape of a horse.

366 Gordon Richards, 26-times champion flat race jockey in Britain, was the first jockey to receive a knighthood.

367 Grey colouring never occurs in the Dartmoor pony.

368 A hippocampus was a fabulous creature like a griffin but with the hind quarters of a horse.

369 Hartwell, Scamperdale and Harry Highover are all types of Pelham bit.

370 Hippotomy is the dissection of the horse.

371 A quadrem is a team of four horses harnessed abreast.

372 The flank is one of the compulsory exercises in the sport of vaulting.

373 In Mongolia there are more horses than humans.

374 The Iceland Horse has a well-developed homing instinct.

375 The foal of a palomino mare and palomino stallion is always palomino in colour.

376 Hippomachy is a fight on horseback.

377 During the Boer War the coats of the Royal Scots Greys horses were dyed chestnut with sodium permanganate for camouflage purposes.

378 Hippocrene was an ancient Greek fountain supposed to have been produced by a stroke of Pegasus's foot.

379 Napoleon Bonaparte's horse Marengo ended his days in retirement in Ireland.

380 Creeping Sally was a famous blind trotting mare who once covered 50 miles of road in 4 hours 45 minutes without breaking from trot.

381 The Kladrub Stud, famous for producing carriage horses, is the oldest stud farm in the world.

382 Genghis Khan, the Mongol emperor, set up a postal courier system using horses.

383 A Murgese is a type of French horse-drawn vehicle.

384 Australian rider Bill Roycroft was 61 years old when he won a team bronze medal at the 1976 Olympics.

385 A jaquima is a type of stirrup.

386 A hippolith is an ancient stone monument built in honour of horses.

387 Tysser's disease is an uncommon, rapidly fatal disease affecting the stomach of young foals.

388 A buckaroo is another name for a bucking bronco.

389 Bishoping means altering the appearance of a horse's teeth in order to disguise its age.

390 Manifesto, winner of the Grand National in 1897 and 1899, ran in the race a record 10 times.

391 A nidget was a triangular horseshoe once used in Kent and Sussex

392 A Dick Christian is a type of jumping saddle.

393 Horses cannot contract the disease anthrax.

394 The individual show jumping title at the 1948 London Olympics was won by a one-eyed horse.

395 A Klibber is a wooden saddle designed for native ponies in the Shetland Isles.

396 Irishman Harry Beasley was—at 83—the oldest jockey ever to ride in a race when he last rode, at Baldoyle in Co Dublin.

397 A capel was a stocky farm horse used in mediaeval times.

398 A hippophagist is someone who eats horsemeat .

399 The great 18th-century racehorse Eclipse won the Epsom Derby by a record 20 lengths.

400 A crinet was a piece of horse armour designed to protect the hind quarters.

?

How Many?

401 How many inches or centimetres are there in a hand?

402 How many riders make up a Pony Club Mounted Games Championship team?

403 In show jumping, how many faults are given for a fence knocked down?

404 Of the nine British breeds of native pony, how many are native to England? Name them.

405 How many sports make up the Pony Club tetrathlon? Name them.

406 How many teeth does an adult female horse normally have in each jaw?

407 In dressage, how many marks are given for a perfect movement?

408 In national show jumping competitions, how many times may a horse or pony fall before being eliminated?

409 How many Pony Club Standards of Efficiency are there?

410 In a three-day event, how many phases of roads and tracks were there?

411 Approximately how many branches of the UK Pony Club are there?
[a] 250
[b] 350
[c] 450

412 How many mouthpieces does a double bridle have?

413 How many four-star three-day events take place annually in Britain? Can you name them?

414 How many riders are there in a horseball team, including substitutes?

415 In show jumping, how many jumps-off are allowed in a Puissance competition?

416 How many times did Lucinda Green win Badminton Horse Trials?

417 How many times did John Whitaker and Milton win the Show Jumping World Cup?

418 How many wheels does the horse-drawn vehicle known as a 'float' have?

419 In showing, how many height divisions are there for children's ridden ponies?

420 At British shows, how many weight divisions are there for ridden show hunters? And name them.

421 In show jumping, how many faults are given for a refusal or run-out?

422 Approximately how many different breeds and types of horses and ponies are there in the world?
[a] 100
[b] 150
[c] 200

423 How many sections of Welsh Pony are there? Name them.

424 In the show jumping world championships, how many riders take part in the individual final where they ride their own and each others' horses?

425 How many equestrian disciplines are included in the Olympic Games? And name them.

426 According to the old rhyme, how many white legs should a horse have for you to 'keep him to the end'?

427 In eventing, how many times may a horse fall on the cross-country before being eliminated?

428 How many 'schools above the ground' are performed by the horses of the Spanish Riding School of Vienna? And name them.

429 How many 'schools on the ground' are performed by the horses of the Spanish Riding School of Vienna? And name them.

430 In international show jumping, how many seconds is a rider allowed after the signal to start is given before the clock starts running?

431 In racing, how many horses take part in a contest known as a match?

432 How many joints does the mouthpiece of a Dr Bristol bit have?

433 How many letter markers are used around the sides of a small (40 x 20-metre) dressage arena? And list them.

434 How many shades of chesnut are recognised in the Suffolk Punch breed?

435 How many times did Arkle win the Cheltenham Gold Cup?

436 How many times did Lester Piggott ride the winner of the Epsom Derby?

437 How many mouthpieces does a Citation bridle have?

438 How many days does it take for a botfly egg to hatch?

439 In showing, how many height divisions are there for hacks?

440 In show jumping, how many penalties are awarded if a fence has to be rebuilt following a disobedience?

441 On average, how many bones are there in a horse's skeleton?
[a] 125
[b] 165
[c] 210

442 How many wheels does a barouche have?

443 In dressage, how many marks are given to indicate that an exercise was executed 'sufficiently'?

444 How many times did Mark Todd win Badminton Horse Trials?

445 About how many breaths per minute does an adult horse take when at rest?

446 In polo, how many minutes are allowed between periods of play to change ponies?

447 A polo match is conducted by how many mounted umpires?

448 At how many miles an hour does the average horse walk?

449 In the 20th century, how many times did Britain win a team gold medal for three-day eventing?

450 In show jumping, what is the minimum number of riders a team must have to compete in a Nations Cup?

451 How many bloodlines does the Lipizzaner breed have? And name them.

452 How many fences do the horses have to jump in the Grand National?

453 How many cervical or neck vertebrae does a horse have?

454 How many tail vertebrae does the average horse have?

455 How many tail vertebrae do Arabian horses have?

456 How many horses were used to pull the type of chariot known as a quadriga?

457 How many sports are run under FEI (Fédération Équestre Internationale) rules? And name them.

458 In the world championships, what distance do endurance horses and riders cover?

459 How many bones are there in a horse's skull?

460 How many small carpal joints make up a horse's knee joint?

461 In horseball, how many consecutive passes involving three different players must be made before a goal may be scored?

462 In the 20th century, how many times did Britain win an Olympic team gold medal for show jumping?

463 How many types of coat pattern occur in the Appaloosa breed? What are they?

464 How many bones are there in a horse's leg?

465 According to modern scientific research, when horses are transported by road or plane for more than 12 hours, how many days do they need to recover from the journey?
[a] 1 to 2
[b] 2 to 3
[c] 3 to 4

466 How many litres of saliva does the average horse secrete each day?

467 How many horses did Aimé Tschiffely take on his famous two-and-a-half-year ride from Buenos Aires to Washington DC?

468 In driving, how many horses form a unicorn or spike?

469 How many ribs does a horse have?

470 At about how many days old does a foal start to nibble solid food?
[a] 8
[b] 12
[c] 16

471 For about how many hours a day does a horse sleep?

472 How many Olympic gold medals did the German dressage rider Dr Reiner Klimke win?

473 On average, how many months does it take for a horse's hoof wall to grow from the coronary band to the toe?

474 How many times can a horse run in the Epsom Derby?

475 How many incisor teeth does a newborn foal have?

476 How many legs did the Norse god Odin's horse Sleipnir have?

477 In October 2008, the Spanish Riding School in Vienna accepted two candidates to train as riders at the school—the first of their kind for nearly 500 years. Who or what were they?
[a] Russians
[b] Women
[c] Roman Catholics

478 How many toes did the modern horse's ancestor, Eohippus, have on its forefeet?

479 How many toes did Eohippus have on its hind feet?

480 Roughly how many years ago did Eohippus live?
[a] 20 million
[b] 37 million
[c] 55 million

481 How many gaits does the Icelandic Horse have? Name them?

482 In the history of the modern Olympic Games, how many riders have won more than one individual gold medal?
And name them.

483 How many horses have won both the Cheltenham Gold Cup and the Champion Hurdle?
And name them.

484 How many types of walk are shown by the Tennessee Walking Horse? And name them.

485 Which political party in the United States of America has the donkey as its symbol?

486 Under Jockey Club Rules, how many hurdles must a horse jump in a two-mile hurdle race?

487 How many chromosomes does the modern horse have?

488 How many distinct patterns of coat colouring occur in the American Paint Horse? And name them.

489 How much does an adult horse's liver weigh?

490 How long is the average horse's oesophagus (or gullet)?

491 How many times did Virginia Leng (née Holgate) win the European Three-day Event Championship?

492 In Britain, how many licensed racecourses are there?
[a] 49
[b] 60
[c] 53

493 How many erythrocytes or red cells does a horse have per cubic millimetre of blood?
[a] 4 million
[b] 6 million
[c] 8 million

494 In the Middle Ages a knight's warhorse had to be capable of carrying the rider, the rider's arms and armour, his saddle and bridle and his own armour. About how many kilograms or pounds would all that have weighed?

495 How many races did the Italian-bred Ribot win in his unbeaten career?

496 In the year 2000 the Irish show jumping team won an all-time record number of Nations Cups. How many?

497 At the 2000 Olympic Games in Sydney, how many marks was Germany's Isabell Werth on Gigolo, the top rider in the team competition, awarded?
[a] 1868
[b] 1888
[c] 1908

498 When galloping, how many feet (or metres) was it estimated that the extraordinary 18th-century Thoroughbred Eclipse covered with each stride?

499 How many letter markers are used around the sides of a large 60 × 20-metre dressage arena? Can you list them?

500 There were an estimated 300,000 horses working in London in the late 19th century. How much manure was it estimated that they produced daily?
[a] 200–300 tons (203.2–304.8 tonnes)
[b] 300–400 tons (304.8–406.4 tonnes)
[c] 400–500 tons (406.4–508 tonnes)

? Which Horse?

501 Mark Todd rode which horse to two successive Olympic three-day event individual gold medals?
[a] Southern Comfort
[b] Charisma
[c] Just An Ace

502 Which breed of horse has the same name as a type of cross-country fence?
[a] Trakehner
[b] Oldenburg
[c] Westphalian

503 George Bowman, Senior drives which horses or ponies?
[a] Penrith Ponies
[b] Westmoreland Walkers
[c] Cumberland Cobs

504 Which horses, in their public displays, perform the movement known as the croupade?
[a] The Cadre Noir
[b] The Spanish Riding School of Vienna
[c] The King's Troop, Royal Horse Artillery

505 Which was the favourite horse of King Richard II?
[a] White Surrey
[b] Black Bess
[c] Roan Barbary

506 Which British native pony has a distinctive mealy coloured nose and toad eyes?
[a] The Exmoor
[b] The Dartmoor
[c] The Dales

507 Only one horse has won two individual Olympic gold medals for dressage. Which one?
[a] Ahlerich
[b] Rembrandt
[c] Gigolo

508 'There may be faster horses, no doubt handsomer, but for bottom and endurance I never saw his fellow.' Which horse was being described?
[a] Red Rum
[b] Copenhagen
[c] Murphy Himself

509 According to an old saying, which horse's mouth should not be examined?
[a] A dark horse
[b] A gift horse
[c] A pale horse

510 Which horse won the 2010 British Jumping Derby at Hickstead?
[a] Promised Land
[b] Softrack Skip Two Ramiro
[c] Mondriaan

511 Which horse's spectacular racing career came to an abrupt end when he broke a pedal bone at Kempton Park?
[a] Desert Orchid
[b] Arkle
[c] Red Rum

512 On which horse owned by HM the Queen did Captain Mark Phillips win Badminton in 1974?
[a] Kilbarry
[b] Columbus
[c] High and Mighty

513 Which present-day horse used to be known as a 'rouncy'?
[a] Hack
[b] Hunter
[c] Cob

514 Which pony won an Olympic show jumping medal in 1968?
[a] Champ VI
[b] Stroller
[c] Dundrum

515 Which American pony breed has Appaloosa colouring?
[a] American Shetland
[b] Pony of the Americas
[c] Chincoteague

516 On which horse did HRH Princess Anne win the European three-day event title in 1971?
[a] Great Ovation
[b] Be Fair
[c] Doublet

517 Which French-bred horse won the Grand National in 2009?
[a] Lean Ar Aghaidh
[b] Mon Mome
[c] Victoire Pour Moi

518 Mary Gordon-Watson was the first woman to become world three-day event champion. Which was her winning ride?
[a] Chicago III
[b] Countryman III
[c] Cornishman V

519 About which great racehorse was it once said '_____ first, the rest nowhere'?
[a] Arkle
[b] Eclipse
[c] Sea Bird II

520 If you spill salt, which coloured horse should you lead through the kitchen to ward off bad luck?
[a] Black or brown
[b] Piebald or skewbald
[c] White or grey

521 Which horse did Ginny Leng give to Ian Stark in exchange for Griffin?
[a] Glenburnie
[b] Stanwick Ghost
[c] Murphy Himself

522 Which breed of pony has a black and silver mane?
[a] Haflinger
[b] Highland
[c] Fjord

523 On which horse did Leslie Law win the three-day event gold medal at the 2004 Athens Olympics?
[a] Shear H20
[b] Shear Water
[c] Shear L'Eau

524 Which breed was dressage rider Kyra Kirklund's famous partner Matador?
[a] Dutch Warmblood
[b] Danish Warmblood
[c] Hanoverian

525 Horses of which breed are crossed with Thoroughbreds to produce excellent polo ponies?
[a] Peruvian Paso
[b] Andalusian
[c] Criollo

526 Which British heavy horse earned the title of 'the breed that built Australia'?
[a] The Clydesdale
[b] The Suffolk
[c] The Shire

527 Which show jumper is the only one to have won a medal at three consecutive Olympic Games?
[a] Halla
[b] Meteor
[c] Ratina Z

528 Which famous American racehorse was known as 'Big Red' because of his fiery chestnut colour?
[a] Kelso
[b] Man o' War
[c] John Henry

529 Which breed of horse, famed for its tremendous endurance and resistance to heat, is bred in Tukmenistan?
[a] The Tersk
[b] The Orlov Trotter
[c] The Akhal-Teke

530 Which horse won the Cheltenham Gold Cup a record five times?
[a] Golden Miller
[b] Arkle
[c] Desert Orchid

531 Which American horse is either a three-gaiter or a five-gaiter?
[a] Missouri Fox Trotter
[b] Morgan
[c] Saddlebred

532 Which native British pony comes from river valleys to the east of the Pennines?
[a] The Highland
[b] The Dales
[c] The Fell

533 Who was Earlsrath Rambler?
[a] A 19th-century racehorse
[b] An international show-jumper ridden by former Pony Club chairman, Dawn Wofford (née Palethorpe)
[c] A leading endurance riding horse of the 1980s

534 Which horse was
Napoleon's charger and
is buried in England, at
Glassenbury Park in
Kent?
[a] Jericho
[b] Jaffa
[c] Jeddah

535 Which colt won the
Epsom Derby in 2010
in a new record time?
[a] Workforce
[b] Jan Vermeer
[c] Midas Touch

536 Which horse, ridden
by Isabell Werth,
won the Grand Prix
Special gold
medal at the 2006
World Dressage
Championships?
[a] Goodman
[b] Ellington
[c] Satchmo

537 Which show jumper
was the first horse
outside racing to win a
million pounds in prize
money?
[a] Boomerang
[b] Milton
[c] Dollar Girl

538 Who was Messenger?
[a] An English
Thoroughbred
stallion who became
the foundation sire
of the Standardbred
racehorse
[b] A famous Pony
Express horse
[c] The mount of one of
Napoleon's generals
at Waterloo

539 Which horses wear
hobbles when they
race?
[a] Trotters
[b] Pacers
[c] Quarter Horses

540 With which breed of
British native pony
is the Linnell strain
associated?
[a] Highland
[b] Fell
[c] New Forest

541 Which horse did the
Duke of Wellington
ride at the Battle of
Waterloo?
[a] Copenhagen
[b] Marengo
[c] Bucephalus

542 Which horse, ridden by Caroline Powell, won the Burghley Horse Trials in 2010?
[a] Lenamore
[b] Apache Sauce
[c] Carousel Quest

543 Which horse is said to 'drink the wind'?
[a] The Arabian
[b] The Barb
[c] The Thoroughbred

544 Which of these famous Oldenburg horses excelled at dressage?
[a] Weihaiwej
[b] Classic Touch
[c] Bonfire

545 Which breed of semi-wild horse lives in the Rhône delta of southern France?
[a] The Ariègeois
[b] The Camargue
[c] The Boulonnais

546 Which horse wears plates?
[a] A show jumper
[b] A racehorse
[c] A wheeler in a team of driving horses

547 Which American horse survived the Battle of Little Big Horn and thereafter lived a life of luxury, with the nickname 'the second Commanding Officer of the Garryowens'?
[a] Comanche
[b] Castor
[c] Carman

548 In John Betjeman's poem *Hunter Trials* which pony, ridden by Prunella, is described as 'the wizardest pony on earth'?
[a] Puzzle
[b] Muzzle
[c] Guzzle

549 Which horses live in semi-wild herds in New Zealand's North Island?
[a] Brumbies
[b] Kaimanawas
[c] Mustangs

550 Which horse was the favourite of Mary Queen of Scots?
[a] Black Agnes
[b] Black Beauty
[c] Black Bess

551 Who were Mancha and Gata?
- [a] Horses ridden by Don Quixote
- [b] The Criollo horses ridden by Aimé Tschiffely from Buenos Aires to Washington DC
- [c] Shetland ponies kept at Windsor Castle and driven by Queen Victoria

552 Which famous American foundation sire was originally named Figure?
- [a] Justin Morgan
- [b] Hambletonian 10
- [c] Allan

553 Which pony-sized breed is always known in its homeland as a horse?
- [a] The Haflinger
- [b] The Fjord
- [c] The Icelandic

554 Horses of which Dutch breed are always black?
- [a] Gelderland
- [b] Friesian
- [c] Groningen

555 Who was Kisber?
- [a] The Hungarian-bred winner of the Epsom Derby in 1876
- [b] The favourite mount of Genghis Khan
- [c] The foundation sire of the Hungarian half-bred horse

556 On which horse did Kristina Cook win bronze in the team and individual three-day event at the 2008 Beijing Olympics, and then gold at the 2009 European Eventing championship at Fontainebleau, France?
- [a] Miner's Frolic
- [b] Minor Relic
- [c] Mighty Rex

557 Which Thoroughbred is generally reckoned to be the first truly great racehorse?
- [a] Flying Childers
- [b] Marske
- [c] Eclipse

558 Which horse won the British Jumping Derby at Hicksted a record four years running during the 1970s?
[a] Mattie Brown
[b] Boomerang
[c] Deister

559 In *The Iliad*, what was the name of Achilles' horse, who had the power of speech?
[a] Xanthos
[b] Xerxes
[c] Artaxerxes

560 Which heavy horse breed is descended from the medieval warhorse known as the 'Great Horse'?
[a] The Shire
[b] The Suffolk
[c] The Percheron

561 Which breed of diminutive horse, 'lost' for many centuries, was re-discovered in northern Iran in 1965?
[a] The Falabella
[b] The Caspian
[c] The Sorraia

562 Riding which horse did Lord Cardigan lead the Charge of the Light Brigade?
[a] Paddy
[b] Dandy
[c] Billy

563 Which of these famous dressage horses was not a Westphalian?
[a] Ahlerich
[b] Rembrandt
[c] Gigolo

564 Which American breed was developed in the rugged Ozark Hills during the 19th century?
[a] Tennessee Walking Horse
[b] Missouri Fox Trotting Horse
[c] The Morgan Horse

565 Which breed of heavy horse is traditionally branded on the neck with an anchor?
[a] Breton
[b] Boulonnais
[c] Ardennais

566 Which ponies live on a sandy island, only 44 km long, in the Atlantic Ocean east of Nova Scotia?
[a] Chincoteague
[b] Galician
[c] Sable Island

567 Which horse of the Roman Emperor Lucius Versus lived in the imperial palace and was fed on almonds and raisins?
[a] Celer
[b] Cyllaros
[c] Cerus

568 Which of these breeds of horse comes from Chile?
[a] Azteca
[b] Campolina
[c] Corralero

569 In Britain during the 19th century, which breed of pony began to be used to haul coal in the mines, replacing human labour?
[a] Fell
[b] Dartmoor
[c] Shetland

570 Which horses are described by the poet Roy Campbell as 'Sons of the Mistral'?
[a] Barb
[b] Camargue
[c] Arab

571 Which horse, ridden by Mary King, fell at the first cross-country fence at Badminton in 1996?
[a] King William
[b] King Boris
[c] Star Appeal

572 Which horse has been bred for several thousand years in the mountain regions of Austria?
[a] Haflinger
[b] Noriker
[c] Marimmano

573 In Scandinavian legend which horse, whose name means 'frost-mane', was the horse of night?
[a] Kantaka
[b] Hrimfaxi
[c] Shibdiz

574 The 1923 FA Cup Final at Wembley is known as 'The White Horse Final' after a mounted police officer drove the huge crowd back to the edge of the pitch so that the football could start. What was his horse's name?
[a] Houdini
[b] Billy
[c] Baldwin

575 Which grey racehorse was affectionately known as Dessie and won the King George VI Chase at Kempton Park four times (1986, 1988, 1989, 1990), as well as the Cheltenham Gold Cup in 1989?
[a] Desert Orchid
[b] Des O'Connor
[c] Destiny's Child

576 The small type of which French heavy horse breed used to be known as 'the fish merchant' because it was used to transport fish from the coast to Paris?
[a] Boulonnais
[b] Percheron
[c] Breton

577 In 1965, on which horse did Australian rider Bill Roycroft finish third behind Arkle in the Cheltenham Gold Cup and, a few weeks later, complete Badminton Horse Trials in sixth place?
[a] Our Solo
[b] Stoney Crossing
[c] Eldorado

578 Which North American breed is often referred to as 'The Little Iron Horse' because of its strength, toughness and tolerance of inclement weather?
[a] Canadian Horse
[b] Morgan Horse
[c] Mustang

579 Who were Flick and Flock?
[a] The last ponies to work in British coal mines
[b] Queen Victoria's favourite driving ponies
[c] Circus horses trained by Elizabeth, Empress of Austria

580 Which horse set an unofficial North American high jump record in 1902 when he cleared 2.515 m (8 ft 3 in) at a public demonstration at his owner's farm in Richmond, Virginia?
[a] Great Heart
[b] Heatherbloom
[c] Confidence

581 In racing, who was the French colt who won the English Triple Crown and became known as 'The Avenger of Waterloo'?
[a] Gladiateur
[b] Allez France
[c] Saint Crespin

582 Which notoriously savage stallion owned by Lord Dorchester was tamed by the famous American horse tamer, John S. Rarey?
[a] Carawich
[b] Crusier
[c] Coady

583 On which horse did Lester Piggott, then aged 18, win his first Epsom Derby?
[a] Gay Time
[b] Zucchero
[c] Never Say Die

584 Which horse owned by Queen Elizabeth II won two English Classic races—the Oaks and the St Leger—in 1977?
[a] Highclere
[b] Dunfermline
[c] Height of Fashion

585 Of which German warmblood breed is the Traventhall Stud considered the birthplace?
[a] Holstein
[b] Hanoverian
[c] Trakehner

586 Cannon Ball, foaled in 1904, is the first stallion listed in which stud book?
[a] Connemara
[b] New Forest
[c] Shetland

587 Who was Sir Barton?
[a] The first American horse to win an Olympic medal
[b] The first winner of the American Triple Crown
[c] The foundation sire of the American Saddlebred

588 Which Epsom Derby winner is buried in the grounds of Easby Abbey at Richmond, in North Yorkshire?
[a] Ellington
[b] Emilius
[c] Empery

589 Whose favourite hunter was called Borysthenes?
[a] Mr Jorrocks
[b] The Emperor Hadrian
[c] Xenophon

590 Which horse, bred in the northern Caucasus in Russia, is well known for its surefootedness over mountainous terrain?
[a] Orlov Trotter
[b] Don
[c] Kabardin

591 Which European heavy horse closely resembles the Suffolk Punch?
[a] Ardennais
[b] Jutland
[c] Belgian Draught

592 Which breed of horse was Dr Le Gear, who was foaled in 1902, stood 21 hh (2.134 m) and weighed just under 27 cwt (1,370 kg)?
[a] Shire
[b] Percheron
[c] Clydesdale

593 Which of these horses is native to Portugal and a close relative of the Andalusian?
[a] Furioso
[b] Lusitano
[c] Maremmano

594 In France, which horses compete for the Prix d'Amerique?
[a] Show jumpers
[b] Steeplechasers
[c] Trotters

595 Which is the only horse to have won Badminton and Burghley Horse Trials and a European show jumping championship?
[a] Merely-a-Monarch
[b] High And Mighty
[c] Great Ovation

596 Which famous British steeplechaser began his racing career by taking a crashing fall at the last hurdle in his very first race and lay on the ground, severely winded, for 12 minutes?
[a] The Dikler
[b] Red Rum
[c] Desert Orchid

597 Who was King Louis XIII of France's favourite horse?
[a] Bonette
[b] Bonite
[c] Boniform

598 Who was the famous
Hungarian racehorse,
unbeaten in all 54 of
her starts in the 1870s,
who always travelled
with her pet cat?
[a] Kisber
[b] Kilgeddin
[c] Kincsem

599 Which British dressage
rider, born in Mainz,
Germany, was ranked in
August 2010 as 3rd in
the world riding Mistral
Hojris and 21st on
Andretti H?
[a] Laura Bechtolsheimer
[b] Imke Schellekens-
    Bartels
[c] Carl Hester

600 On which horse did
Becky Hart of the USA
win three consecutive
Endurance World
Championships in 1988,
1990 and 1992?
[a] Czar Louis
[b] Dancing Queen
[c] R.O. Grand Sultan

? Sporting Chance

601 What is the maximum permitted height for a pony in Pony Club mounted games?
[a] 13.2 hh (137 cm)
[b] 14 hh (142.2 cm)
[c] 14.2 hh (148 cm)

602 What is a triple bar?
[a] A type of show jumping fence
[b] Part of the undercarriage of a horse-drawn vehicle
[c] Three refusals at the same cross-country fence

603 In which sport do competitors perform one-time changes?
[a] Endurance riding
[b] Dressage
[c] Reining

604 Who ride across Luckington Lane?
[a] Competitors at Blenheim Horse Trials
[b] Competitors at Burghley Horse Trials
[c] Competitors at Badminton Horse Trials

605 How old must a pony be to take part in Pony Club mounted games?
[a] 4 years old
[b] 5 years old
[c] 6 years old

606 In carriage driving, how many penalties are incurred for knocking down a cone in the final phase?
[a] 5
[b] 10
[c] 15

607 How many teams qualify for the Prince Philip Cup mounted games final at NEC Arena in Birmingham?
[a] 5
[b] 6
[c] 7

608 Who was the first woman to train the winner of the Grand National?
[a] Jenny Pitman
[b] Henrietta Knight
[c] Venetia Williams

609 What is the normal length of time of a chukka in Pony Club polocrosse?
[a] 4 minutes
[b] 6 minutes
[c] 8 minutes

610 Which of these sports is not an Olympic discipline?
[a] Show jumping
[b] Endurance riding
[c] Dressage

611 In show jumping, how many refusals incur elimination?
[a] 2
[b] 3
[c] 4

612 In which sport do horses negotiate hazards?
[a] Carriage driving
[b] Endurance riding
[c] Harness racing

613 In which sport is use of the voice forbidden?
[a] Dressage
[b] Carriage driving
[c] Polo

614 In preliminary and novice level dressage, which types of walk must competitors produce?
[a] Medium
[b] Medium and freé
[c] Medium and extended

615 In dressage, what does the mark 7 for a movement signify?
[a] Satisfactory
[b] Fairly good
[c] Good

616 What is a *concours d'élégance*?
[a] A Western riding competition
[b] A driving competition
[c] A dressage competition

617 Who was the first eventing rider to win the World Championship twice?
[a] Bruce Davidson
[b] Virginia Leng
[c] Blyth Tait

618 What is a stepping stone dash?
[a] Another name for a quarter horse race
[b] A mounted game
[c] A type of equine coat marking

619 Who competes in a Prix St Georges competition?
[a] A dressage rider
[b] A junior show jumping rider
[c] An endurance rider

620 Where would you find an obstacle called a keyhole?
[a] On a carriage driving marathon course
[b] On a show jumping course
[c] On an eventing cross-country course

621 Which British showground is famous for the Derby Bank and Devil's Dyke?
[a] Windsor
[b] Harrogate
[c] Hickstead

622 In which sport is the ball fitted with leather handles?
[a] Polo
[b] Polocrosse
[c] Horseball

623 In show jumping, how many faults are incurred if a horse puts one or more feet into a water jump?
[a] None
[b] 3
[c] 4

624 Where would you see riders perform a serpentine?
[a] In a dressage arena
[b] On a polo ground
[c] On a racecourse

625 What is an arrowhead?
[a] A movement in vaulting
[b] A team manouevre in polocrosse
[c] A narrow cross-country fence

626 How old do horses have to be to compete at Badminton?
[a] At least 5 years old
[b] At least 8 years old
[c] At least 7 years old

627 How many types of walk are recognised in dressage? Name them.
[a] 2
[b] 3
[c] 4

628 The Australian-born event rider Matt Ryan now competes for which country?
[a] USA
[b] Canada
[c] Great Britain

629 In bending races, how far apart are the poles positioned?
[a] 4.5–7.3 m (5–8 yd)
[b] 6.4–9.1 m (7–10 yd)
[c] 8.2–11 m (9–12 yd)

630 When was the Prince Philip Cup for mounted games introduced?
[a] 1957
[b] 1967
[c] 1977

631 In which sport are competitors required to perform sliding stops?
[a] Dressage
[b] Reining
[c] Horseball

632 In foxhunting, what is the 'line'?
[a] The huntsman's whip
[b] The members of the field waiting outside a covert
[c] The trail of the fox

633 In which sport did HRH Princess Haya bint Al Hussein represent Jordan in the 2000 Olympic Games?
[a] Show jumping
[b] Polo
[c] Dressage

634 What is Le TREC?
[a] Pony trekking in France
[b] Junior endurance riding
[c] A competition for leisure riders comprising orienteering, basic riding control and cross-country

635 The Boomerang Trophy is awarded to the winner of which competition?
[a] The British Jumping Derby
[b] The Melbourne Cup
[c] The Tom Quilty Ride

636 Which modern equestrian sport is thought to have originated in Persia nearly 3,000 years ago?
[a] Dressage
[b] Polo
[c] Steeplechasing

637 Between what ages must a rider be to compete in the Pony European Championships?
[a] 10–14
[b] 12–16
[c] 14–16

638 Who won the 2001 European Dressage Championship?
[a] Ulla Salzgeber and Rusty
[b] Nadine Capelmann and Farbenfroh
[c] Isabell Werth and Anthony FRH

639 In dressage, at what level do competitors need to show the first degrees of collection and medium canter?
[a] Preliminary
[b] Novice
[c] Elementary

640 In dressage, how many marks are awarded for position and seat of rider and correct use of the aids?
[a] 10
[b] 15
[c] 18

641 Crossing and foul hooking are infringements of the rules in which sport?
[a] Horseball
[b] Carriage driving
[c] Polo

642 In flat racing, the Lincoln Handicap is held at which racecourse?
[a] Lingfield Park
[b] Lincoln
[c] Doncaster

643 In mounted games, what happens if a rider breaks a bending pole?
[a] The race is restarted
[b] The rider carries on and completes the race without penalty
[c] The rider is eliminated

644 What was extraordinary about the 1993 Grand National?
[a] It was abandoned because of waterlogged ground
[b] All the runners fell
[c] It was declared void because of a false start

645 What is the minimum number of fences permitted in a Puissance jump-off?
[a] 1
[b] 2
[c] 3

646 In which sport did American actress Stefanie Powers compete?
[a] Show jumping
[b] Polo
[c] Dressage

647 What is Capability's Cutting?
[a] A hazard on the Windsor carriage driving marathon course
[b] An obstacle on the Burghley Horse Trials cross-country course
[c] An obstacle on the Kentucky Three-Day cross-country course

648 Which racecourse has also held the (motor racing) British Grand Prix?
[a] Goodwood
[b] Aintree
[c] Doncaster

649 In polo, which players are a team's forwards?
[a] Numbers 1 and 2
[b] Numbers 2 and 3
[c] Numbers 1 and 3

650 Who was the first woman to race ride under National Hunt rules?
[a] Meriel Naughton
[b] Jane Thorne
[c] Marie Tinkler

651 Who was the first woman to win a gold medal in the open show jumping World Championships?
[a] Liz Edgar
[b] Leslie McNaught-Mandli
[c] Caroline Bradley

652 The Rowley Mile at Newmarket is named after a famous horse called Old Rowley owned by which English monarch?
[a] King Charles II
[b] Queen Anne
[c] King Edward VII

653 Which famous racehorse's owner's colours are green with red epaulets?
[a] Sheikh Mohammed
[b] The Aga Khan
[c] HM The Queen

654 In which hand is it permitted to hold a polo stick?
[a] Left
[b] Right
[c] Either

655 When was the dressage freestyle to music competition first included in the Olympic Games?
[a] Barcelona in 1992
[b] Atlanta in 1996
[c] Sydney in 2000

656 Who is or was a renowned driver of Hackney teams?
[a] Karen Bassett
[b] George Bowman, Senior
[c] Cynthia Haydon

657 What takes place at Prestbury Park?
[a] Cheltenham Races
[b] The Pony Club Polo Championships
[c] The Great Yorkshire Show

658 Who were not allowed to ride in the Olympic three-day event competition until 1956?
[a] Women
[b] Non-commissioned military officers
[c] Riders under the age of 25

659 Which sport includes cutting, trail and pleasure competitions?
[a] Western riding
[b] Endurance riding
[c] Carriage driving

660 Who had a fall on the flat and rode the second half of the three-day event cross-country course at the Atlanta Olympic Games with a broken collarbone?
[a] Individual silver medallist Sally Clark on Squirrel Hill
[b] Team gold medallist Gillian Rolton on Peppermint Grove
[c] Team bronze medallist Vicky Latta on Broadcast News

661 In February 2009, for the first time ever in the UK, a 20 Goal arena polo test match took place. Where?
[a] Hurlingham Park
[b] Windsor
[c] Hickstead

662 Where did the sport of horseball originate?
[a] USA
[b] France
[c] Germany

663 In flat racing, what is the shortest distance raced over in Britain?
[a] 5 furlongs
[b] 6 furlongs
[c] 7 furlongs

664 Who was the first woman to ride a winner under National Hunt rules?
[a] Ann Ferris
[b] Diana Thorne
[c] Gee Armytage

665 Who receives an Armada Dish?
[a] A rider who completes Badminton Horse Trials three times
[b] A rider who completes Badminton Horse Trials five times
[c] A rider who completes Badminton Horse Trials seven times

666 If you were using a Smithwick Devil's Horse, in what sport would you be taking part?
[a] Rowing
[b] Gymnastics
[c] Fishing

667 In foxhunting, what is an unentered hound?
[a] A hound who has never hunted
[b] A hound who has not finished one cub-hunting season
[c] A hound who has not killed a fox

668 Which show jumping competition has a course that comprises two distinct sections?
[a] Double Accumulator
[b] Fault and Out
[c] Power and Speed

669 Who is the only horse ever to have officially opened the Commonwealth Games?
[a] Bounce
[b] Charisma
[c] Ready Teddy

670 Which nation won silver and bronze medals in the individual dressage competition at the 2008 Olympic Games in Beijing?
[a] Russia
[b] Holland
[c] Germany

671 Who was the first-ever three-day event rider to win four different 4-star competitions?
[a] Oliver Townend
[b] Pippa Funnell
[c] William Fox-Pitt

672 In dressage, what is a volte?
[a] A 6-metre circle
[b] A 10-metre circle
[c] A 20-metre circle

673 Who was the first woman to win a three-day event Olympic gold medal?
[a] Mary Gordon-Watson
[b] Bridget Parker
[c] Jane Holderness-Roddam [née Bullen]

674 In foxhunting, what is a skirter?

[a] A hound who cuts corners instead of following the true line of a fox

[b] A side-saddle rider

[c] A non-mounted follower

675 Which show jumping family fielded an entire team during the 2001 Nations Cup season?

[a] The Whitakers of Great Britain

[b] The Millars of Canada

[c] The Beerbaums of Germany

676 Whose 100-mile (160 km) ride in California in 1955 led to the formation of the modern sport of endurance riding?
[a] Tom Quilty
[b] Wendell T. Robie
[c] Lloyd Tevis

677 Which champion Australian racehorse was shot at by gunmen on the morning of the 1930 Melbourne Cup, escaped unhurt, won the race in the afternoon but later died in mysterious circumstances in America?
[a] Carbine
[b] Phar Lap
[c] Peter Pan

678 Which non-European is the only rider to have won the European Show Jumping Championship?
[a] Nelson Pessoa
[b] Rodrigo Pessoa
[c] William Steinkraus

679 Which future Show Jumping World Cup winner won the Junior European Championship in 1970?
[a] John Whitaker
[b] Jos Lansink
[c] Markus Fuchs

680 The Dubai World Cup was the world's single richest horse race in 2010. What was the total prize money?
[a] US$ 10,000,000
[b] US$ 12,000,000
[c] US$ 8,000,000

681 Which horse completed Badminton Horse Trials seven times?
[a] Get Smart
[b] Ballycotton
[c] Murphy Himself

682 Apart from Golden Miller, which other horse won both the Cheltenham Gold Cup and the Grand National?
[a] Team Spirit
[b] L'Escargot
[c] Corbiere

683 Who was the last rider
to win an international
three-day event with a
bonus score?
[a] Richard Meade
[b] Lucinda Green
[c] Ian Stark

684 Where and what is the
Red Mile?
[a] A flat-race course in
southern Australia
[b] A famous harness
raceway at Lexington
in Kentucky
[c] A racecourse for
Arabian horses in
Dubai

685 What record did event
rider Virginia Leng set
in 1986?
[a] First rider to win
Badminton Horse
Trials four years
running
[b] First rider to win
the European
Championship three
times running
[c] First rider to win
Burghley Horse Trials
four years running

686 Who set the official
world Puissance
record of 2.40 m
(7 ft 10½ in)
in 1991?
[a] Nelson Pessoa on
Miss Möet
[b] Franke Sloothaak on
Leonardo
[c] Otto Becker on
Lausbub

687 Which legendary
British football pundit
was taught to ride by
Liz and Ted Edgar and
became an enthusiastic
rider to hounds?
[a] Jimmy Hill
[b] David Coleman
[c] John Motson

688 Who, in 1974, became
the first British rider
since 1914 to win
the Grand Pardubice
Steeplechase in
Czechoslovakia?
[a] Lord Oaksey
[b] Bill Shand-Kidd
[c] Chris Collins

689 Only one horse has won both the King George V Gold Cup and the Queen Elizabeth II Cup at the Royal International Horse Show. Which one?
[a] Pennwood Forge Mill
[b] Sunsalve
[c] Milton

690 When do the Pan American Games take place?
[a] Annually except for Olympic years
[b] Every two years between the Olympic Games and the World Equestrian Games
[c] Once every four years in the year before the Olympic Games

691 Who was the first woman to ride in an Olympic three-day event?
[a] Mary Gordon-Watson
[b] Lana Dupont
[c] Jane Holderness-Roddam (née Bullen)

692 Which sport uses a mobile starting gate?
[a] Flat racing
[b] Harness racing
[c] Endurance riding

693 In Sweden, which equestrian sport attracts bigger crowds than football?
[a] Harness racing
[b] Carriage driving
[c] Show jumping

694 Who has been appointed to design the three-day event course for the 2012 Olympic Games in London?
[a] Mike Etherington-Smith
[b] Sue Benson
[c] Hugh Thomas

695 Which British television commentator was also a Master of Foxhounds and hunted the former Olympic event horse Sea Breeze?
[a] Raymond Brooks-Ward
[b] Dorian Williams
[c] Peter O'Sullivan

696 In Western riding, what is the movement where a horse stops from a gallop, turns 180 to left or right and immediately gallops away?
[a] Spin
[b] Pirouette
[c] Rollback

697 Which former three-time National Hunt Champion Jockey competed in the 2009 series of television show, Strictly Come Dancing?
[a] Richard Dunwoody
[b] Bob Champion
[c] Peter Scudamore

698 Who was the first woman to jump a clear round in the Hamburg Jumping Derby?
[a] Pat Smythe
[b] Kathy Kusner
[c] Marion Mould

699 In Canadian cutting horse competitions, how many penalty points are incurred by a horse who bites the cattle?
[a] 3
[b] 5
[c] 7

700 At the 2006 World Single Horse Championships, who won the individual title for Britain?
[a] HRH The Duke of Edinburgh
[b] Paul Sidwell
[c] Georg Bowman, Senior

Where?

701 Where should you stand to pick up a horse's foreleg?
[a] By his shoulder, facing his head
[b] By his shoulder, facing his tail
[c] Facing his shoulder

702 Where is the Festival of British Eventing held, which includes the British Eventing British Open Championship?
[a] Bramham
[b] Gatcombe
[c] Blenheim

703 Where can you feel a horse's pulse?
[a] On his withers
[b] On his lower jaw
[c] On his pastern

704 When bandaging a horse's leg, where should you fasten the tapes?
[a] Front of the leg
[b] Outside of the leg
[c] Inside of the leg

705 Where would you see an anti-weaving grille?
[a] On a loom
[b] On a headcollar
[c] On a stable door

706 Where would you expect to see an overreach?
[a] In a show jumping arena when a horse takes off too far from a fence
[b] On the heel of a horse's forefoot
[c] In a horse's mouth

707 Where would you find bog spavins?
[a] On a waterlogged hunter trial course
[b] In hay
[c] On the joint capsules of a horse's hock

708 Where, according to an old saying, should you never change horses?
[a] At the opening meet
[b] In mid-stream
[c] At the bottom of a hill

709 Where would you find roundings?
[a] On a Pelham bridle with a single rein
[b] In a bag of coarse mix
[c] On a horseshoe

710 Where on a horse would you find an ergot?
[a] Inside his ear
[b] On his stifle
[c] At the back of his fetlock joint

711 In Robert Browning's poem, where did Dirck and his companions gallop to bring the good news?
[a] From London to Brighton
[b] From Calais to Paris
[c] From Ghent to Aix

712 Where does the Royal International Horse Show take place?
[a] Hickstead
[b] Wembley
[c] Peterborough

713 Where do Connemara ponies come from?
[a] Scotland
[b] Ireland
[c] Italy

714 Where are the UK headquarters of the Pony Club?
[a] London
[b] Stoneleigh
[c] Cirencester

715 Where would you put a buckle guard?
[a] On your spur straps
[b] On the harness of your riding hat
[c] On the girth straps of your saddle

716 Where were the 2010 FEI World Equestrian Games held?
[a] Stockholm
[b] Aachen
[c] Kentucky

717 Where are a horse's sesamoid bones?
[a] In his feet
[b] Behind his fetlock joints
[c] In his skull

718 **Where would you put a wooden cradle?**
[a] In a mare and foal's stable
[b] In a jumping grid
[c] Round a horse's neck

719 **Where would you find a lip strap?**
[a] On a polo helmet
[b] On a horse who gets his tongue over the bit
[c] On a bridle with a curb chain

720 **Where would you find garter straps?**
[a] On a pair of breeches
[b] On a pair of riding boots
[c] On the flaps of a saddle

721 **Where do botfly larvae generally live?**
[a] In a horse's large intestines
[b] On a horse's lower legs
[c] In a horse's stomach

722 **Where would you find treads?**
[a] On a horsebox ramp
[b] On a stable floor
[c] On stirrup irons

723 **Where on a horse would you find feather?**
[a] On his forehead
[b] On his ears
[c] On his legs

724 **Where would you see a treble combination?**
[a] In a betting shop
[b] In a carriage driving competition
[c] On a show jumping course

725 **Where are you likely to see Windsor Greys?**
[a] In an artist's studio
[b] In British state processions
[c] In a riding wear shop

726 **Where do redworms live?**
[a] In a horse's large intestines
[b] In a horse's small intestines
[c] In a horse's lungs

727 **Where do grass cracks occur?**
[a] On a horse's hoof, from the wearing surface upwards
[b] On a horse's hoof, from the coronet downwards
[c] On the sole of the horse's foot

728 **Where is the English village after which the great show jumper Milton was named?**
[a] In Warwickshire
[b] In Northamptonshire
[c] In Leicestershire

729 **Where would you see a placing pole?**
[a] At the start of a bending race
[b] In a dressage arena
[c] On the take-off side of a practice fence

730 **Where is Germany's national training centre?**
[a] Hamburg
[b] Düsseldorf
[c] Warendorf

731 **On post and rail fencing, for safety where should the posts be?**
[a] On the outside of the fence, furthest away from the horse
[b] On the inside of the fence
[c] On either side alternately

732 **Where might you find a 'prophet's thumb mark'?**
[a] On a saddle
[b] On a horse's hoof
[c] On a horse's neck

733 **Where would you fit a bib?**
[a] To the headcollar of a stabled horse to prevent him biting his clothing
[b] To the front of a riding coat to keep your knees dry
[c] To a carriage horse's bridle to prevent him from grazing

734 Where does bran come from?
   [a] It is a by-product of wheat
   [b] It is a by-product of oats
   [c] It is a by-product of barley

735 In which county are the headquarters of the British Horse Society?
   [a] Buckinghamshire
   [b] Worcestershire
   [c] Warwickshire

736 Where is a horse's patella?
   [a] In his knee
   [b] In his fetlock
   [c] In his stifle

737 Where does the Golden Horseshoe Ride take place?
   [a] Dartmoor
   [b] The New Forest
   [c] Exmoor

738 Where is the UK's National Horseracing Museum?
   [a] Newmarket
   [b] Lambourn
   [c] Liverpool

739 Where would you see breeching?
   [a] On a harness horse
   [b] On a rider's legs
   [c] On a steeplechase course

740 Where were the Scottish Horse Trials Championships held until 2008?
   [a] Burgie
   [b] Thirlestane Castle
   [c] Blair Castle

741 Where is a horse's Achilles tendon?
   [a] In his foreleg
   [b] In his hind leg
   [c] A horse does not have an Achilles tendon

742 Exmoor ponies have ranged freely on a wild expanse of moorland in South West England for thousands of years. Where exactly is Exmoor?
   [a] In South Devon
   [b] In West Devon
   [c] In West Somerset and North East Devon

743 In Walter de la Mare's poem *The Huntsman*, where did three jolly gentlemen in coats of red ride their horses?
[a] Up the road
[b] Up the hill
[c] Up to bed

744 Where would you find a quarter mark?
[a] On the horn of a horse's hoof
[b] On the polo field
[c] On a horse's hind quarters

745 In the 19th century, where did Colonel Przewalsky discover wild horses?
[a] Poland
[b] Russia
[c] Mongolia

746 Where on a horse is the area known as the poll?
[a] Immediately in front of his withers
[b] Between his ears
[c] Between his eyes

747 Where would you find a fly-link?
[a] On a fly fringe
[b] On a curb chain
[c] On a carriage

748 Where did the first-ever Royal Festival of the Horse take place in July 2010?
[a] Stoneleigh
[b] Harrogate
[c] Peterborough

749 Where was the Horse of the Year Show held before it moved to the NEC in Birmingham?
[a] Wembley Arena
[b] Royal Albert Hall
[c] Earl's Court

750 Where would you find a caulkin?
[a] On a horse's body underneath the saddle
[b] On a New Zealand rug
[c] On a horseshoe

751 Where in France does the Percheron horse come from?
[a] Brittany
[b] Normandy
[c] Provence

752 Where would you find a rigging dee?
[a] On a Western saddle
[b] On a set of breast harness
[c] On a farrier's apron

753 Where are a horse's coccygeal vertebrae?
[a] In his back
[b] In his tail
[c] In his neck

754 Where is the Scottish Grand National run?
[a] Perth
[b] Kelso
[c] Ayr

755 Where would you expect to find chorioptic mange?
[a] On a horse's fetlocks and pasterns
[b] On a horse's hind quarters
[c] Round a horse's eyes

756 Where was the first steeplechase run?
[a] At Liverpool
[b] On the outskirts of London
[c] In County Cork

757 Where would you find a splinter bar?
[a] On a horse-drawn vehicle
[b] On a horseshoe
[c] In American-style barn stabling

758 Where can you see the remains of the ancient racetrack known as the Circus Maximus?
[a] Athens
[b] Rhodes
[c] Rome

759 Where would you hear the term 'all on'?
[a] In the hunting field
[b] At a trekking centre
[c] At a driving meet

760 Where is the Animal Health Trust based?
[a] Newmarket
[b] Bristol
[c] London

761 Where on a horse would you see ermine marks?
[a] Surrounding his eye
[b] Surrounding his coronet
[c] On his nostrils

762 Where is the Crabbet Park Stud, famous for its Arabian horses?
[a] Suffolk
[b] Cumbria
[c] Sussex

763 Where is a horse's lingual canal?
[a] In his mouth
[b] In his nose
[c] In his ear

764 Where are the headquarters of the Cadre Noir?
[a] Versailles
[b] Saumur
[c] Bordeaux

765 Where would you find a Kornakoff?
[a] At a Russian stud farm
[b] On a stirrup leather
[c] In a horse's mouth

766 Where would you find triangular tables?
[a] In a restaurant
[b] On a cross-country course
[c] On a horse's teeth

767 Where is the famous showground known as the Piazza di Siena?
[a] Madrid
[b] Rome
[c] Lisbon

768 Where is a horse's pisiform bone?
[a] At the back of his knee
[b] At the back of his hock
[c] At the back of his fetlock

769 According to Harrison Ainsworth's novel *Rockwood*, where did the highwayman Dick Turpin ride on his mare Black Bess?
[a] From Edinburgh to Newcastle
[b] From Bristol to London
[c] From London to York

770 Where are the headquarters of World Horse Welfare (which was formerly known as the International League for the Protection of Horses)?
[a] Norfolk
[b] London
[c] The Hague

771 Where is the historic showground called Ballsbridge?
[a] Edinburgh
[b] Exeter
[c] Dublin

772 Where did the Charge of the Light Brigade take place?
[a] Waterloo
[b] Balaclava
[c] Austerlitz

773 Where are the Horseshoe Falls?
[a] Canada
[b] Iceland
[c] Switzerland

774 Where is a horse's common digital extensor muscle?
[a] In his lower foreleg
[b] In his forearm
[c] In his shoulder

775 Where did the British army lose half a million horses?
[a] Waterloo
[b] The Boer War
[c] The First World War

776 Where did the Emperor Charlemagne's horse cause a famous city to be founded after he unearthed a spring by pawing the ground?
[a] Aachen
[b] Paris
[c] Vienna

777 Where is the Horse River?
[a] Idaho, in the USA
[b] Alberta, in Canada
[c] Queensland, in Australia

778 Where in the 20th century were perfectly preserved 2,500-year-old horses' bodies discovered in frozen tombs?
[a] In the Alps
[b] In Alaska
[c] In Siberia

779 Where was the final of the Show Jumping World Cup held in 2008?
[a] Switzerland
[b] USA
[c] Germany

780 Where would you find a horse called a Kathiawari, which has inward-pointing ears?
[a] In Egypt
[b] In Mexico
[c] In India

781 Because of quarantine restrictions, the equestrian events of the 1956 Olympic Games in Melbourne could not be staged in Australia. Where were they held?
[a] Helsinki
[b] Stockholm
[c] Rome

782 Where did Attila the Hun believe no grass would ever grow again?
[a] Where his horse's hoof had stepped
[b] On the ground where he died
[c] Where his enemies' horses died in battle

783 Where would you find an agister?
[a] In a saddler's shop
[b] On a horse's fetlock
[c] In the New Forest

784 Where could John Jorricks' horse Arterxerxes often be seen?
 [a] Being driven in tandem behind his stablemate Xerxes
 [b] Upside down in a ditch
 [c] Galloping home alone

785 Where in England is there a custom that every peer who passes through the town for the first time must either leave a shoe from his horse or pay a fine?
 [a] Oakham, in Rutland
 [b] Horseway, in Cambridgeshire
 [c] Shoebury Ness, in Essex

786 Where would a piece of armour known as a bardel have been worn?
 [a] On a rider's right arm
 [b] On a rider's lower leg
 [c] On a horse's breast and flanks

787 Where is Europe's premier flat race, the Prix de l'Arc de Triomphe, run?
 [a] Chantilly
 [b] Longchamp
 [c] Vincennes

788 Where in the Bible are the Four Horsemen of the Apocalypse described as riding a white, red, black and pale horse?
 [a] *Psalms*
 [b] *Proverbs*
 [c] *Revelation*

789 Where is there a statue of the Duke of Wellington on Copenhagen, cast from the metal from captured French guns?
 [a] At Waterloo
 [b] Opposite the Royal Exchange in London
 [c] In front of Blenheim Palace

790 Where is the Kentucky Derby run?
 [a] Churchill Downs
 [b] Belmont Park
 [c] Laurel Park

791 Where could you see O'Donohue's white horses?
[a] The Lakes of Killarney
[b] Punchestown racecourse
[c] At Dublin Horse Show

792 Where was unbeaten racehorse Ribot bred?
[a] The Pompadour Stud in France
[b] The Spendthrift Stud in the United States
[c] The Dormello Stud in Italy

793 From where did the people of ancient China import their much-prized 'celestial horses'?
[a] India
[b] Burma
[c] Persia

794 Where did nomadic horsemen traditionally carry their supply of meat?
[a] In a saddle bag
[b] In their pockets
[c] Under their saddles

795 Where are the horse latitudes?
[a] On the equator
[b] About 10° north and south
[c] About 30° north and south

796 Where is the Flyinge Stud?
[a] Norway
[b] Denmark
[c] Sweden

797 Where would you see a housen?
[a] In a stable yard
[b] On a draught horse's collar
[c] In a hunt kennels

798 In 19th-century America, where did Pony Express riders carry the mail?
[a] Between St Joseph in Missouri and Sacramento in California
[b] Between Dallas in Texas and Sacramento
[c] Between Denver in Colorado and Sacramento

799 Where would you find
   a hardie hole and a
   beak?
   [a] On a farrier's anvil
   [b] On a plough horse's
       harness
   [c] In a loriner's
       workshop

800 At Asbyrgi there is a
   giant horseshoe-shaped
   indentation in the
   ground said to have
   been made when Odin's
   horse, galloping across
   the skies, stumbled
   and put down his foot.
   Where is Asbyrgi?
   [a] Lapland
   [b] Iceland
   [c] Greenland

?

How and Why?

801 How can you estimate a horse's age?
[a] By the appearance of his teeth
[b] By the shape of his feet
[c] By his height

802 How should carrots be fed to horses?
[a] Sliced lengthways
[b] Sliced in rings
[c] Cut into cubes

803 For safety, about how wide should a horse's stable door be?
[a] 91.5 cm (3 ft)
[b] 106.5 cm (3 ft 6 in)
[c] 122 cm (4 ft)

804 Why should you never feed lawn mowings to horses?
[a] They taste nasty
[b] They make them thirsty
[c] They are likely to cause colic

805 How can you test a horse for shoulder lameness?
[a] Observe him in the stable to see if he points his foot
[b] Move his leg and watch for signs of pain
[c] Watch for lameness in the opposite hind leg

806 Why is it not a good idea to feed hay from a hayrack?
[a] The horse has to eat in an unnatural position
[b] The hay will taste of metal
[c] The horse might injure his teeth on the bars

807 Why should you regularly change the diagonal when riding at rising trot?
[a] So that you do not become stiff on one side
[b] So that you do not cause uneven wear on your saddle
[c] So that the horse makes equal use of the muscles on both sides of his body

808 How should sugar beet be fed to horses?
[a] Dry
[b] Well soaked in water
[c] Dampened with a little water

809 Why is it a good idea to graze cattle and sheep with horses?
[a] They attract flies that would otherwise irritate horses
[b] They ingest and destroy parasites that are harmful to horses
[c] They prevent horses from galloping about and injuring themselves

810 Why should the inside of a horse's ears never be clipped?
[a] His hearing might be damaged by the noise of the clippers
[b] The skin is too sensitive
[c] The hair is a natural protection against flies, parasites and foreign objects

811 How can you prevent an exercise sheet from blowing up off a horse's back?
[a] Tie it to his tail
[b] Sew weights to the edge
[c] Fit a fillet string

812 Why should chocolate-based titbits never be fed to competition horses?
[a] They might give them diarrhoea
[b] They contain banned substances
[c] They damage their teeth

813 How can you adjust stirrups to approximately the correct length before you mount?
[a] Take them off the saddle and measure against your legs
[b] Measure legs and leathers with a tape
[c] Put your knuckles on the stirrup bar of the saddle and adjust the leathers so that the irons reach your armpit

814 Why would you use a crupper?
[a] To prevent a horse from kicking
[b] To prevent your saddle from slipping forwards
[c] To make a horse carry his tail higher

815 How does an eggbut snaffle differ from a loose-ring snaffle?
[a] It has fixed cheeks
[b] It has two sets of rings
[c] The mouthpiece is thicker

816 Why should horses who are prone to sweet itch be stabled at daybreak and nightfall?
[a] Because that is when the biting midges which cause it are most active
[b] Because that is when most people have time to apply medication
[c] Because that is when horses most like to sleep

817 Why should you never kneel on the ground when bandaging a horse's leg?
[a] You cannot get out of the way quickly if he moves
[b] You might hurt your knees
[c] You will dirty your clothes

818 Why should you wear gloves when lungeing a horse?
[a] To keep your hands clean
[b] To keep your hands warm
[c] To protect your hands against rope burns

819 How should stable bandages be applied?
[a] On all four legs without padding underneath
[b] On all four legs over a layer of padding
[c] Only on the forelegs, never the hind legs

820 Why should you never wear earrings, noserings and other jewellery when riding?
[a] It is not considered good etiquette
[b] You might lose them
[c] They can cause serious injury if they become entangled

821 How should a cavesson noseband be fitted?
[a] As close as possible to the projecting cheek bones
[b] One finger's width below the projecting cheek bones
[c] Two fingers' width below the projecting cheek bones

822 Why should you never wet a tail bandage before use?
[a] It might make the horse cold
[b] It might shrink and restrict his blood circulation
[c] Dye from the fabric might stain his tail

823 How should Pony Club members dress for the riding phase of the Tetrathlon?
[a] As for eventing dressage
[b] As for eventing cross-country
[c] As for eventing show jumping

824 How would you describe a grey horse whose coat has light circular patches on a darker background?
[a] Dappled
[b] Iron
[c] Flea-bitten

825 How should you make a turn when leading a horse?
[a] Walk directly in front of his head
[b] Walk beside him and let him walk around you
[c] Walk beside him and turn him away from you so that you stay on his outside

826 Why is it customary to hog the manes of polo ponies?

[a] To give the grooms less work

[b] To prevent a rider grabbing hold of an opponent's pony

[c] To prevent the rider's stick getting caught up

827 How can you help to prevent the habit of box walking?

[a] Keep the horse tied up all the time

[b] Give the horse a very deep straw bed

[c] Give the horse toys to play with

828 When preparing for a dressage test, why is it best to practise the movements separately rather than repeating the whole test?

[a] So you won't get bored

[b] So the horse won't get bored

[c] So the horse won't anticipate the movements

829 Why is it important to remove droppings from a horse's field?

[a] It prevents unpleasant smells

[b] It makes the field look tidier

[c] It helps to reduce worm infestation

830 When leading a young horse, why is it better to use a coupling attachment than to fasten the lead rein directly to the bit ring?

[a] It looks more professional

[b] It stops him swinging round and biting you

[c] It helps to prevent the horse's mouth becoming one-sided

831 How can a farrier cure or prevent a capped elbow?

[a] By removing the horse's shoes

[b] By fitting a seated-out shoe

[c] By fitting a shoe with a short, narrow inner heel

832 In the UK, why are horses not usually clipped later than early February?
[a] The coat has stopped growing by then
[b] The quality of the summer coat will be poor
[c] February is cold

833 How can you detect on which side a horse is lame 'behind'?
[a] His hip will drop when his sound limb strikes the ground
[b] His hip will drop when his lame limb strikes the round
[c] His head will drop when his sound limb strikes the ground

834 When using a numnah, why should you push it well up into the front arch and channel of the saddle?
[a] To prevent strain on the centre seam
[b] To prevent it pressing on the horse's backbone
[c] To prevent it slipping

835 How would you recognise the early stages of strangles?
[a] The horse has a sore throat and finds it difficult to swallow
[b] The horse drinks continuously
[c] The horse suffers from nosebleeds

836 Why do horses groan?
[a] Because they are angry
[b] Because they are ill or in pain
[c] Because they want to attract the attention of their friends

837 How can an assistant help to keep a horse still while he is being clipped?
[a] By tickling his ears
[b] By singing to him
[c] By holding up a foreleg

838 How is the horse's os pedis more commonly known?
[a] The hoof
[b] The coffin bone
[c] The pastern

839 How would you describe informal hunting dress worn during cub-hunting?
[a] Cubbing clothes
[b] Half-hunters
[c] Rat-catcher

840 How can you quickly remove sweat or water from a horse's coat?
[a] With a sponge
[b] With a sweat-scraper
[c] By encouraging the horse to roll

841 How can you teach a horse not to rush his fences?
[a] Change to a stronger bit
[b] Fit a standing martingale
[c] Go back to grid work

842 Why is sheep netting unsuitable for fencing horse paddocks?
[a] It looks very unattractive
[b] A horse might get his feet tangled in it
[c] Horses chew it

843 Why would you use a poll-guard?
[a] To protect a horse's head when travelling
[b] To keep a horse's head warm and dry when exercising in bad weather
[c] To prevent a competition horse being distracted

844 Why are leather gloves unsuitable for riding in wet weather?
[a] Your reins will slip through them
[b] The colour may wash off on to your hands
[c] They will not keep your hands warm

845 According to the nursery rhyme, why would you ride a cock-horse to Banbury Cross?
[a] To see a young lady upon a black horse
[b] To see a fine lady upon a white horse
[c] To see an old lady upon a grey horse

846 Why would a horse wear a coronet boot?
[a] As a decoration on ceremonial occasions
[b] To make his action higher and more showy
[c] To protect him from overreach injuries

847 In hunting, how would you describe two foxes?
[a] A brace
[b] A couple
[c] A pair

848 Why would a veterinary surgeon use a stethoscope on a horse?
[a] To examine the eyes
[b] To listen to the heart, lungs and gut
[c] To look down the throat

849 How would you describe a horse who has scars on his knees?
[a] Broken-down
[b] Broken-kneed
[c] Broken-jointed

850 How would you describe a white patch between a horse's nostrils?
[a] Snip
[b] Stripe
[c] Splash

851 How can you tell if a horse is dehydrated?
   [a] Offer him a bucket of water and see how quickly he drinks it
   [b] Pinch a fold of skin on his neck and see if it springs back to normal within a second
   [c] Examine his mouth for signs of dryness

852 How can you teach a horse not to veer to one side when he is jumping?
   [a] Jump him alongside another, straight-going horse
   [b] School him over crossed-pole fences to steer him towards the middle
   [c] Hit him down the shoulder on take-off

853 How does a Kineton noseband work?
   [a] It exerts pressure on the horse's nose
   [b] It helps to keep a horse's mouth closed
   [c] It exerts pressure on the horse's poll

854 Why would you use a Chifney bit?
   [a] To lead a strong horse, particularly one who is inclined to rear
   [b] To lead a horse who bites
   [c] To lead a horse who carries his head very low

855 Why does a bar shoe help in the treatment of weak heels and corns?
   [a] It provides a good foothold
   [b] It transfers weight from the heels onto the frog
   [c] It allows the hoof wall to expand

856 Why are excessively long pasterns not desirable in a riding horse?
   [a] They are inclined to be weak
   [b] They give a jarring ride
   [c] Horses with long pasterns are prone to laminitis

857 Why should you not lean to the side of your horse's neck every time you take a jump?

[a] You will strain your back

[b] You will unbalance the horse

[c] Your jacket will get dirty

858 Why is a fence with a good ground-line easier for a horse to jump than one without?

[a] Because it makes the fence appear smaller

[b] Because it makes the fence look more solid

[c] Because the horse judges his take-off point from the ground-line

859 When lungeing, how can you use the whip to help keep a horse out on the circle?

[a] Direct it towards his hind quarters

[b] Flick it towards his head

[c] Point it towards his shoulder

860 How did Federico Caprilli change the course of horsemanship?

[a] He invented the stirrup

[b] He introduced the forward seat

[c] He invented the sport of show jumping

861 How can you encourage a reluctant horse to go into a horsebox?

[a] Ride him up the ramp

[b] Attach a lunge-rein to the side of the vehicle and use it to apply pressure above his hocks

[c] Get several helpers to stand behind him and make a lot of noise

862 Why might you use a half-halt?

[a] To adjust your horse's balance by putting more weight on his hind quarters

[b] To prepare your horse for a movement

[c] To stop your horse rushing forward

863 In show jumping, if a rider decides to retire before the end of a round how should he signal his decision to the judges?
[a] By cantering straight out of the arena
[b] By raising his whip or hand
[c] By circling twice and then halting

864 How did Yankee Doodle come to London?
[a] On an old gray mare
[b] Riding on a pony
[c] Sitting astride as gentlemen ride

865 How do you describe a racehorse who finishes unplaced?
[a] Out of form
[b] Off the pace
[c] Also ran

866 How would you describe a spotted horse whose coat is white with spots of any colour?
[a] Snowflake
[b] Leopard
[c] Blanket

867 Why would you fit large, square studs in your horse's shoes?
[a] To give extra grip on roads
[b] To give extra grip onhard going
[c] To give extra grip in muddy ground

868 In eventing, how does a CIC differ from a CCI?
[a] A CIC is for junior riders, a CCI for seniors
[b] A CIC is a one-day event, a CCI is a three-day event
[c] A CIC is a national competition, a CCI is an international competition

869 Why are calf-knees (knees which deviate backwards) a bad conformational fault?
[a] They place undue strain on the ligaments at the back of the carpus
[b] They give a very uncomfortable ride
[c] They look unattractive

870 Why would you give a horse electrolytes?
[a] To prepare him for worming
[b] To prevent colic
[c] To replace body salts lost during strenuous exercise

871 How is the condition known as knuckling or 'over at the fetlock' caused?
[a] A parasitic infection
[b] A horse repeatedly knocking his front feet when jumping
[c] Contraction of the tendons of the digital flexors

872 Why is Lascaux in the Dordogne Valley of France of interest to horsemen?
[a] For its ancient, well-preserved cave paintings of horses
[b] For the stud farm where the Selle Français horse was first bred
[c] For being the home of the Cadre Noir

873 Why do some show jumping horses wear a stomach shield?
[a] To prevent them injuring themselves with their studs when they fold their front legs
[b] To encourage them to jump higher
[c] To keep them clean

874 How does a horse's eyesight differ from a human's?
[a] A horse can't see colours
[b] A horse can see almost all round himself without turning his head
[c] A horse can't see in the dark

875 Why is the horse chestnut tree so-named?
[a] The leaves are horseshoe-shaped
[b] It was once believed that the tree's seeds would cure abroken-winded horse
[c] Traditionally, its wood was used to make saddle trees.

876 Why is the plant horse-vetch so called?
[a] It has horseshoe-shaped pods
[b] It is appetising to horses
[c] It cures horses of colic

877 How would you recognise synovial fluid?
[a] It looks like water
[b] It is clear and straw-coloured, like thin honey
[c] It is thick and orange-coloured

878 Why are Palomino horses so named?
[a] The word 'palomino' is Spanish for 'golden'
[b] They are named after the Mexican Count de Palomino who was presented with a gold-coloured horse by the Spanish explorer Cortés
[c] It was the name given to the first horse of that colour, owned by Queen Isabella

879 Why, in 1978, did Jennie Lorison-Clarke enter the record books?
[a] She became the first British rider to win a dressage medal
[b] She became the first British rider to compete in the dressage World Championships
[c] She became the first rider to win the British national dressage title 10 times

880 Having been selected to ride for Britain at both the 2004 and 2008 Olympic Games, Zara Phillips was forced to withdraw from the three-day event. Why?
[a] Her horse, Toytown, was injured in training
[b] Her grandmother, HM The Queen, forbade her from riding
[c] She broke her arm on both occasions

881 How was the American Pony Express rider and showman William Frederick Cody better known?
[a] Elephant Bill
[b] Buffalo Bill
[c] Chief Sitting Bull

882 Why is the Grand National fence known as 'The Chair' so named?
[a] It is shaped like a chair
[b] The jockey of the first horse to jump it was unseated and left sitting on top of the fence
[c] An iron chair used to be placed by the jump for the distance judge to sit on

883 In the song *Waltzing Matilda*, how did the squatter ride up to the jolly swagman?
[a] Mounted on a Thoroughbred
[b] Trotting on a stockhorse
[c] Sitting on a one-eyed mule

884 Why is magnesium an important mineral in a horse's diet?
[a] It aids the correct functioning of muscle, bone, teeth and enzyme systems
[b] It transports oxygen from the lungs to the tissues
[c] It is required for cartilage formation

885 How does this 17th-century quotation finish: 'England is the paradise of women, the purgatory of men, and…'?
[a] The heaven of horses
[b] The hell of horses
[c] The haven of horses

886 The Holy Roman Emperor Charles V said he spoke Spanish to God, Italian to women and French to men. How did he speak to his horse?
[a] In English
[b] In German
[c] In Dutch

887 According to Hindu tradition, how is the chariot of the Sun God drawn?
[a] By one winged horse
[b] By two horses
[c] By eight horses

888 How many countries has show jumper Peter Charles represented in international competitions?
[a] One
[b] Two
[c] Three

889 How did the famous equestrian painter John Frederick Herring earn his living as a young man?
[a] As a jockey
[b] As a huntsman
[c] As a stage coachman

890 How do American flat-racecourses differ from those in the UK?
[a] They do not have starting stalls
[b] They are all left-handed
[c] They have a downhill finish

891 Why did the 'heavenly horses' of the Chinese Emperor Wu appear to sweat blood?
[a] Their necks and hind quarters were traditionally decorated with vegetable dye which, when the horses sweated, looked like drops of blood
[b] A parasite beneath the skin caused slight bleeding which coloured the horses' sweat
[c] Their dappled coat-colouring gave the appearance of flecks of blood

892 Why did the ancient Chinese have such an important effect upon modern carriage driving?
[a] They invented the wheel
[b] They invented breast harness
[c] They invented metal horseshoes

893 In Stephen Butler Leacock's *Nonsense Novels*, how did Lord Ronald ride?
[a] Badly
[b] Back to front
[c] Madly off in all directions

894 Why was the horse first domesticated?
[a] For use as a beast of burden
[b] For use as a riding animal
[c] To provide milk and meat

895 How would you be travelling if you went on Shanks's pony?
[a] On a donkey
[b] On a farm cart
[c] On foot

896 In olden times, why would a horse have worn a peytral?
[a] To protect his chest in battle
[b] To prevent him from biting his neighbour
[c] To protect his feet

897 How does a carriage driver give or return a salute?
[a] By raising his hat
[b] By nodding his head
[c] By raising his whip hand to face-level

898 Why is 648 BC an important date in the history of horsemanship?
[a] It is said to be the date of the invention of the stirrup
[b] It was the first year in which mounted horsemen competed in races at the Olympic Games
[c] It was the year in which the first riding academy was founded

899 How would a horse suffering from bracken poisoning be treated?
[a] Thiamine (vitamin B_1)
[b] Liquid paraffin
[c] There is no known cure

900 Why are the letters K, F, V, P, E, B, S, R, H and M used around a dressage arena?
   [a] Because they are easy to distinguish from a distance
   [b] They are said to be based on the letters used on the stable yard walls at the old Imperial German Court to indicate where each horse was to stand while waiting for his rider
   [c] They were drawn out of a hat when the first dressage test was written

? Mixed Bag

901 What is a sliphead?
[a] The bridoon strap on a double bridle
[b] A quick-release safety device found on driving harness
[c] A horse who repeatedly removes his headcollar

902 In dressage, how does the piaffe differ from the passage?
[a] Piaffe is a four-beat gait
[b] There is no forward movement in piaffe
[c] In piaffe the legs move in lateral, not diagonal, pairs

903 What is meant by the term 'over-tracking'?
[a] When a horse's hind feet step beyond the hoofprints of his forefeet
[b] When a three-day event rider takes the wrong course on Phase A
[c] When a gateway becomes churned up and muddy

904 What is a star gazer?
[a] A horse with poor eyesight
[b] A horse who refuses to concentrate on his work
[c] A horse who holds his head very high

905 Where would you find a kick bolt?
[a] On the front of a horse-drawn carriage
[b] On a horse's hind shoes
[c] On the bottom of a stable door

906 What does 'being carted' mean?
[a] Being stretchered away after a bad fall
[b] Travelling by horse and cart
[c] Being run away with

907 Which part of the horse's body regulates the blood and controls the nutrients carried in it?
[a] The heart
[b] The pancreas
[c] The liver

908 Who are said always to get their man?
[a] The Royal Canadian Mounted Police
[b] New York City Mounted Police
[c] City of London Police

909 What is a melanoma?
[a] A tumour of the eye
[b] A bony growth on the coronet
[c] A tumour of the skin

910 What is a Balding girth?
[a] A folded leather girth
[b] A plaited leather girth
[c] An elasticated girth

911 What is fullering?
[a] A term used to describe a groove in the ground surface of a horseshoe
[b] A term used to describe the feeding of hounds
[c] A term used to describe the decorative leather on a Western saddle

912 What are keepers?
[a] People who care for hounds
[b] Loops on saddlery through which straps are passed
[c] Metal buckles

913 What are billets?
[a] Temporary stables for horses at shows
[b] Fastenings at the ends of reins and cheek pieces
[c] Fees for keeping horses at livery

914 In eventing in the UK, which item of dress is obligatory for the cross-country?
[a] A jacket
[b] Gloves
[c] A body protector

915 Who said: 'A good trainer can hear a horse speak to him. A great trainer can hear him whisper'?
[a] Monty Roberts
[b] Kyra Kirklund
[c] Nelson Pessoa

916 What is a Witney blanket?
- [a] A quarter sheet used for winter exercising
- [b] A type of sweat sheet
- [c] A gold-coloured under-blanket with black and red stripes

917 What, on a horse, is the atlas?
- [a] The first cervical veterbra
- [b] The skull
- [c] The base of the neck

918 What is the piece of leather that covers the stirrup bar on a saddle called?
- [a] Saddle flap
- [b] Buckle guard
- [c] Skirt

919 Who has an 'armchair seat'?
- [a] A very small child
- [b] A rider who sits on the back of the saddle with his legs pushed forward
- [c] The driver of a four-in-hand

920 Who is the only rider to have won two successive European Three-Day Event Championships on the same horse?
- [a] Lucinda Green on George
- [b] Pippa Funnell on Supreme Rock
- [c] Mark Phillips on Columbus

921 Which is the best and safest metal for making stirrup irons?
- [a] Nickel
- [b] Stainless steel
- [c] Aluminium

922 What are grass reins?
- [a] Cross-over reins attached to the saddle to prevent a pony putting his head down to graze
- [b] Soft, plaited reins made from hemp
- [c] Long leading reins used when exercising a horse who cannot be ridden

923 What should all
horses and ponies be
inocculated against?
[a] Typhoid
[b] Malaria
[c] Tetanus

924 Who would wear a
feather-edged shoe?
[a] A side-saddle rider
[b] A horse who
brushes
[c] A horse with
abundant hair on his
lower legs

925 Who or what is a
horsewalker?
[a] A mechanical device
for exercising horses
[b] A groom who
handles stallions at
stud
[c] An apprentice jockey

926 What is a zebroid?
    [a] A prehistoric zebra
    [b] A cross between a male horse and a female zebra
    [c] A cross between a male zebra and a female horse

927 In a jump-off for which show jumping competition is an optional practice fence provided inside the arena?
    [a] A Nations Cup
    [b] A Puissance
    [c] A Top Score

928 What is a false quarter?
    [a] A defect of the hoof wall
    [b] A badly fitted hind shoe
    [c] A foxhound who does not hunt with the pack

929 What is the King's Troop part of?
    [a] The Royal Bodyguard
    [b] The Royal Horse Artillery
    [c] The Royal Household

930 What is the meaning of the expression 'to put the cart before the horse?'
    [a] To give a horse an impossible task
    [b] To reverse the natural or proper order of things
    [c] To make a stupid mistake

931 Which character in Lewis Carroll's *Alice Through the Looking Glass* fell off in front whenever his horse stopped, fell off behind whenever it went on again and every now and then fell off sideways?
    [a] The White Knight
    [b] The White King
    [c] The Red King

932 What do the initials RDA stand for?
    [a] Riding and Driving Association
    [b] Regional Dressage Association
    [c] Riding for the Disabled Association

933 What is a cutting horse?
   [a] A racehorse with low galloping action
   [b] A whipper-in's horse
   [c] A cow pony trained to 'cut out' selected animals from a herd

934 What is 'tubbing'?
   [a] Giving a horse a bath
   [b] Immersing a horse's injured foot in warm water
   [c] Making a bran mash

935 Where might you find 'keys'?
   [a] On a huntsman's saddle
   [b] On a mounted drum horse's bridle
   [c] On a mouthing bit

936 What are sidebones?
   [a] Splints on the outsides of horse's knees
   [b] False bones caused by hardening of the cartilages of the pedal bones
   [c] Growths on the coronet

937 What is a bascule?
   [a] A low horse-drawn carriage suitable to be driven by children
   [b] The rounded shape of a jumping horse as he clears the summit of an obstacle
   [c] A French riding school

938 Where on a horse is the seat of curb?
   [a] In his mouth
   [b] On his chin
   [c] A few inches below the point of his hock

939 For a horse in light work, what percentage of his feed ration should be protein?
   [a] 5–6%
   [b] 7.5–8.5%
   [c] 9.5–10.5%

940 What is strapping?
   [a] A thorough grooming of a horse
   [b] A slang word for tack and harness
   [c] The practice of standing up a horse with his front and hind legs stretched out

941 What is a bit guard?
- [a] A security device in a tack room
- [b] A device fitted around the mouthpiece of a bit to prevent chafing
- [c] A type of equine muzzle

942 What is a Segundo?
- [a] A Spanish maker of stirrup irons
- [b] In Italy a spare horse out hunting
- [c] A type of curb bit

943 What is molasses?
- [a] Soaked sugar beet
- [b] Unrefined black treacle
- [c] Flaked maize

944 Which is the highest British Horse Society qualification?
- [a] FBHS
- [b] BHSI
- [c] BHSII

945 Who wrote the novel *The Horse Whisperer*?
- [a] Nicholas Evans
- [b] Nicholas Pileggi
- [c] Dick Francis

946 In racing, what does 'spread a plate' mean?
- [a] A shoe has become loose
- [b] Time for a tea break
- [c] Have a gamble on several runners in the same race

947 What has a head, a neck, a shank and a point?
- [a] A horse's stifle joint
- [b] A lungeing whip
- [c] A horseshoe nail

948 What is the usual treatment for ringbone?
- [a] Antibiotics
- [b] Plenty of exercise
- [c] Rest and anti-inflammatory drugs

949 What is a zonkey?
- [a] A rickety donkey cart
- [b] A cross between a zebra and a donkey
- [c] A slang name for an equine sedative

950 What is the common name for the condition called urticaria?
- [a] Broken wind
- [b] Tying up
- [c] Nettle rash

951 Who wrote the book
Travels in a Donkey Trap?
[a] Enid Blyton
[b] Stella Benson
[c] Daisy Baker

952 What is keratitis?
[a] Inflammation in the
hoof
[b] Inflammation of the
cornea of the eye
[c] Inflammation of the
ear

953 Whose golden chariot
can still be seen in a
famous museum?
[a] Tutankhamen's
[b] Julius Caesar's
[c] Darius's

954 Who were the first
horse and rider to
jump a double
clear round in an
Olympic Nations
Cup?
[a] Foxhunter and
Colonel Harry
Llewellyn
[b] Touch of Class and
Joe Fargis
[c] Robin Z and Peter
Eriksson

955 What is an Australian
Simplex?
[a] A type of lungeing
cavesson
[b] A type of safety
stirrup iron
[c] A type of bitless
bridle

956 A capriole is a high
school air above the
ground. What does the
word capriole mean?
[a] Merry caper
[b] Big jump
[c] Leap of the goat

957 What is pirplasmosis?
[a] Equine leukemia
[b] A tick-borne equine
disease causing fever
and weakness
[c] Sunburn of the
nostrils

958 According to tradition,
which is the luckiest
horseshoe?
[a] One cast from the
winner of the Grand
National
[b] One made of silver
[c] One cast from the
near-hind leg of a
grey mare

959 What is a visor?

[a] A pair of blinkers with a slit in each eye shield

[b] A hood which completely covers the horse's head

[c] A type of fly fringe

960 What is or was a 'boater'?

[a] A straw riding hat once popular in India

[b] A barge horse

[c] A horse being transported on the deck of a ship

961 Who was Stonewall Jackson?

[a] A designer of cross-country courses

[b] A 19th-century cricketer

[c] An American cavalry general

962 In heraldry, what is a horse argent?

[a] A rearing horse

[b] A horse with head bowed

[c] A white horse

963 Who wrote: 'There is no secret so close as that between a rider and his horse?

[a] Alois Podhajsky in *My Horses, My Teachers*

[b] R.S. Surtees in *Mr Sponge's Sporting Tour*

[c] Rudyard Kipling in *The Maltese Cat*

964 What is colostrum?

[a] The first milk produced by a mare after she has given birth to a foal

[b] The main protein of skin, tendon, bone, cartilage and connective tissue

[c] The membrane lining the eyelids

965 What is the White Horse of Uffington?

[a] An old breed of draught horse

[b] A horse cut into a chalk hillside in Oxfordshire

[c] A ghostly horse who appears annually at Halloween

966 In which film did Jane Holderness-Roddam (née Bullen) and her Badminton and Burghley Horse Trials winner Warrior appear as 'doubles' for the stars?
[a] *National Velvet*
[b] *Champions*
[c] *International Velvet*

967 Who wrote the novel *Airs Above the Ground*?
[a] Josephine Pullein-Thompson
[b] Mary Stewart
[c] Susan Hill

968 What was a post horse?
[a] A horse entered for a competition after the official closing date for entries
[b] A carriage horse let out for hire to the public
[c] A spare coach horse attached to the rear of a vehicle by a lead rope

969 Depression, difficulty in swallowing, regurgitation of stomach contents down the nostrils and absence of gut movement are all symptoms of which equine disease?
[a] Tetanus
[b] Strangles
[c] Grass Sickness

970 What is the UK equivalent of the American term 'paddling'?
[a] Overreaching
[b] Forging
[c] Dishing

971 What are Dartnell reins?
[a] Plaited cotton cord reins
[b] Plaited leather reins
[c] Rubber-covered reins

972 Which part of a horse is affected by lampas?
[a] The soft palate
[b] The hard palate
[c] The larynx

973 Who was Benjamin Latchford?
   [a] A famous 19th-century maker of bits
   [b] A famous 19th-century coachman
   [c] A famous 19th-century highwayman

974 What is a mare's nest?
   [a] A hoax or fraud
   [b] A very untidy room
   [c] A broodmare's stable

975 What is the common name for metacarpal periostitis?
   [a] Broken knees
   [b] Capped hocks
   [c] Sore shins

976 What is a Yakut?
[a] An exceptionally hardy breed of horse living in northern Siberia
[b] A leather bottle of Mongolian mare's milk
[c] A heavy blanket used by Russian troika drivers

977 Who toured Britain on horseback and wrote a book entitled *Rides Round Britain*?
[a] John Evelyn
[b] John Byng, Viscount Torrington
[c] John Galsworthy

978 What is hyposodonty?
[a] Having no teeth
[b] Having diseased teeth
[c] Having long teeth

979 Which organism causes the equine disease known as strangles?
[a] Streptococcus equi
[b] Rhodococcus equi
[c] Bordetella bronchiseptica

980 What, in horses, is coprophagia?
[a] The eating of straw bedding
[b] The eating of dung
[c] The chewing of the bark of trees

981 Lester Piggott was the first teenage jockey to ride 100 winners in the UK. Who was the second?
[a] Pat Eddery
[b] Willie Carson
[c] Lanfranco 'Frankie' Dettori

982 Who or what was Remington?
[a] An inventor of typewriters
[b] An American painter and sculptor
[c] A type of horse-drawn carriage

983 Who composed a piece of music called *The Harmonious Blacksmith*?
[a] Handel
[b] Mozart
[c] Beethoven

984 What is unusual about Windsor and Fontwell racecourses?
[a] Both are bounded by rivers
[b] Both only run evening meetings
[c] Both are in the shape of a figure-of-eight

985 Who wrote the poem *The Village Blacksmith*?
[a] Alfred, Lord Tennyson
[b] Henry Wadsworth Longfellow
[c] W.H. Auden

986 What is a shabrack?
[a] A broken down old hunter
[b] A military saddle cloth
[c] A building for storing carriages

987 Which renowned British artist painted a picture entitled *A Country Blacksmith disputing upon the Price of Iron*?
[a] Stubbs
[b] Turner
[c] Constable

988 When was the Grand National first broadcast on radio?
[a] 1927
[b] 1948
[c] 1960

989 Which English place name means 'enclosure or river meadow where horses are kept'?
[a] Stadhampton, Oxfordshire
[b] Horsforth, West Yorkshire
[c] Fersfield, Norfolk

990 Which equine parasite uses mud snails as an intermediate host in its life cycle?
[a] The tapeworm
[b] The liver fluke
[c] The redworm

991 In which work by Sir Walter Scott is a woman robbed and has horseshoes nailed to her feet?
[a] *Rob Roy*
[b] *The Tales of a Grandfather*
[c] *The Bride of Lammermoor*

992 What is the meaning of the expression 'Money will make the mare go'?
[a] If you drop the price, you will sell the horse
[b] If you bribe the jockey, the horse will win the race
[c] If only you have the money, you can do anything

993 The 1844 winner of the Epsom Derby was disqualified when it was discovered that he was a 'ringer'—a four-year-old substitute for the real horse. What was the name of the three-year-old he replaced?
[a] Run And Skip
[b] Running Rein
[c] Run The Gauntlet

994 Who wrote The Lady Who Rides to Hounds, in which it is asserted that 'Women who ride, as a rule, ride better than men'?
[a] Anthony Trollope
[b] R.D. Blackmore
[c] D.H. Lawrence

995 What is or was a prairie schooner?
[a] A comfortable riding horse used by early European settlers in America
[b] A covered, horse-drawn wagon used by pioneers crossing the North American prairies
[c] A drinking bottle attached to a cowboy's saddle

996 The Spanish Narragansett foundation stallion Falcon Rowdy is said to have been the fastest gaited horse ever. What speed did he record in a four-beat gait?
[a] 30 mph
[b] 35 mph
[c] 40 mph

997 What is the oldest recorded age for a Thoroughbred racehorse?
[a] 35
[b] 42
[c] 48

998 In which book does Jem Merlyn go to a horse fair and sell a pony he has stolen to the wife of the person he stole it from?

[a] *Tess of the D'Urbevilles* by Thomas Hardy

[b] *Jamaica Inn* by Daphne du Maurier

[c] *Nerve* by Dick Francis

999 In which sport is the Prix de Cornulier the top award?

[a] French steeplechasing

[b] French dressage

[c] French ridden trotting racing

1000 What was the original title of the Shire Horse Society?

[a] The English Cart Horse Society

[b] The Great Horse Society

[c] The British Draught Horse Society

1001 According to tradition, what titbit proves irresistible to horses who are difficult to catch?

[a] Fennel-flavoured gingerbread

[b] Peppermint-flavoured cake

[c] Comfrey-flavoured biscuits

? Answers

Take Your Pick

1   [b]   *Black Beauty*

2   [c]   Shetland

3   [a]   NEC, Birmingham

4   [c]   In a horse's mouth

5   [c]   The legs

6   [b]   Dressage

7   [b]   At the back

8   [c]   Refuses to do what its rider asks

9   [b]   North America

10   [c]   In his hoof

11   [b]   Ornaments for draught horses

12   [c]   A girth

13   [a]   A palfrey

14   [b]   A horse who drops food from his mouth while eating

15   [c]   40–45

16   [b]   *The Welsh Pony and Cob Society Stud Book*

17   [b]   Someone who knows all about horse care

18   [a]   A Thoroughbred

19   [a]   Part of a horseshoe

20   [b]   A worthless, common horse

21   [b]   North Africa

22   [b]   Half brothers

23   [a]   Quarters-out

24   [c]   A breed of wild horse believed to be an ancestor of the modern horse

25   [c]   Coarse and vulgar

26   [b]   A type of bitless bridle

27   [a]   Rudyard Kipling

28   [b]   The best bet of the day

29   [a]   1948

30   [b]   Leonardo da Vinci

31   [c]   40–50 litres of material

32   [c]   Holland

33   [b]   Yew

34   [a]   Six years old

35   [b]   Bruce Davidson

36   [b]   A worn-out horse

37   [c]   An extra horse used to help teams pull heavy loads up hills

38   [a]   Nick Skelton (riding Lastic, cleared 2.32 m (7 ft 7in. 5/16th)

39   [a]   The Trakehner

40   [c]   A type of schooling martingale

41   [a]   A wedge-shaped pad filling the hollow behind a horse's heels

42   [c]   A farrier

43   [b]   Ignoring them

44   [c]   The Master of the Horse

45   [b]   An injury to the inside of a horse's leg caused by a blow from the opposite foot.

46   [c]   About 4½ miles

47   [b]   In high-school riding

48   [a]   To prevent a horse catching his teeth in the straps

49   [a]   The Scarteen

50   [c]   A short, sharp gallop

51   [b]   The St Leger

52   [c]   A cowboy

53   [a]   George John Whyte-Melville

54   [c]   Random

55   [a]   Spurs

56   [c]   Lillie Langtry

57   [c]   8.40 m (27 ft 6 ¾ in) (set by André Ferreira of South Africa in 1975, riding Something)

58   [a], [b] and [c]

59   [a]   An eye-cover used on the heads of excitable horses to keep them quiet

60   [b]   Egg-bar

61   [c]   From Buenos Aires to Washington

62   [b]   Chantilly

63   [a]   The Nez Percé

64   [a]   The Dartmoor

65   [c]   Trotting irregularly

66   [b]   *Richard III*

67   [a]   A racing sulky

68   [a]   A very big fence

69   [a]   The Kentucky Derby, the Preakness Stakes and the Belmont Stakes

70   [b]   H.H. Dixon

71   [c]   The Hamburg Jumping Derby course

72   [b]   A reduction in the weight carried by a horse ridden by an apprentice

73   [c]   1834

74   [c]   A two-wheeled horse-drawn carriage

75   [b]   600

76   [a]   Mange

77   [b]   A type of early conveyance used by women

78   [a]   John Ruskin

79   [b]   Whooping cough

80   [c]   The seventh year

81   [a]   A type of bridle

82   [a]   Covering the frame of a coachman's seat

83   [b]   A two-horse chariot

84   [a]   The Suffolk

85   [b]   Babolna

86   [a]   The name of a famous trotting horse

87   [b]   Anthony Trollope (*Can You Forgive Her?*)

88   [c]   John Skeaping

89   [c]   Sir Alfred Munnings

90   [a]   Federico Grisone

91 [b] King George III's
92 [b] Bits
93 [b] The Maryland
        Hunt Cup
94 [a] Harness Racing
95 [b] Lord George Bentinck
96 [a] Henry Alken, Senior
97 [b] The Oaks
98 [c] Gigs
99 [b] The Cleveland Bay
100 [a] John Keats

Who's Who?

101 [b] A loriner
102 [a] Tom Smith's
103 [b] A farrier
104 [c] A.P. ('Tony') McCoy
        on Don't Push It
105 [b] Vaulters
106 [a] St Hubert
107 [c] Elizabeth of Austria
108 [b] Alois Podhajsky
        (former director of
        the Spanish Riding
        School of Vienna)
109 [a] Paul Tapner on
        Inonothing
110 [b] Neptune
111 [b] William Funnell
112 [a] HM The Queen
113 [c] Lucy Glitters
114 [a] John Masefield

115 [b] Elizabeth Taylor
116 [a] A veterinary surgeon
117 [c] Only hunt servants
        and officials
118 [b] A cowboy
119 [a] The most famous
        animal painter
        of his day
120 [b] A side-saddle rider
121 [c] The field master
122 [b] A postillion
123 [c] A wheelwright
124 [c] The Trojans
125 [a] Edward Gal on
        Moorlands Totilas
126 [a] Becalmed sailors
127 [a] The riders of the
        Spanish Riding School
        of Vienna (founded
        by the Emperor)
128 [c] The Romans
129 [a] Hinrich Romeike
        on Marius
130 [b] Geraldine Rees
131 [c] HRH The Princess Royal
132 [b] Andrew Hoy
133 [a] Meredith Michaels-
        Beerbaum on
        Shutterfly
134 [a] A leading British
        polo player
135 [a] Dorothy Brooke
136 [a] Merely-a-Monarch and
        Anneli Drummond-Hay

137 [a] Ian Millar

138 [a] A farrier

139 [b] Ellen Whitaker

140 [b] A walker

141 [c] Pat Smythe (who won team bronze in 1956)

142 [b] Walter Swinburn

143 [a] Paul Revere

144 [a] Count Alexis Orlov

145 [b] Alwin Schockemöhle

146 [c] Rustum (who fatally wounded his own son, Sohrab, in Matthew Arnold's poem *Sohrab and Rustum*)

147 [c] A 20th-century Portuguese riding master

148 [b] Phaeton

149 [b] Black Beauty

150 [a] Mark Todd (on Bertie Blunt in 1995)

151 [a] Blacksmiths

152 [c] Fred Archer

153 [c] Raimondo and Piero d'Inzeo (Rome, 1960)

154 [b] The 18th-century riding master François Robichon de la Guérinière

155 [b] Richard the Lionheart

156 [c] Petruchio in *The Taming of the Shrew*

157 [b] Dr Samuel Johnson

158 [a] Muriel Wace, known as 'Golden Gorse'

159 [a] Hartwig Steenken

160 [c] RS Summerhays

161 [c] George Bernard Shaw

162 [b] HRH Princess Haya Bint Al Hussein

163 [a] A saddle or harness maker

164 [a] Fred Winter (on Mandarin)

165 [c] William Cavendish, first Duke of Newcastle

166 [c] William III

167 [b] Polo players

168 [a] Jonathan Swift

169 [b] Sweden

170 [b] John Parker

171 [c] 'Mad Jack' Mytton,

172 [c] James Ward

173 [a] Death

174 [b] The 17th-century riding master Antoine de Pluvinel

175 [a] Rachel Bayliss on Gurgle The Greek (who at the Stockholm fence went under the pole instead of jumping it)

176 [c] Pony Express Riders in America

177 [a] Miguel de Cervantes in *Don Quixote*

178 [a] Adam Lindsay Gordon 1833-1870

179 [b] Renowned riders who founded the Schumann Circus specialising in equestrian acts

180 [a] Racing manager to four British monarchs (and known as 'The Father of Racing')

181 [a] The Emperor Augustus

182 [b] The Neapolitan Prince

183 [b] Peter Beckford

184 [a] Captain Robert Byerley, owner of The Byerley Turk

185 [c] Andrew Marvell

186 [c] The Conquistador Hernando Cortés

187 [a] Cynisca, sister of Agesilaus, King of Sparta

188 [c] Ben Jonson

189 [a] Donald 'Ginger' McCain

190 [c] Condemned prisoners on their way to be hanged at Tyburn.

191 [a] William Blake

192 [b] Imogen

193 [c] The guard on a Royal Mail coach. (It was his coach horn.)

194 [c] Mary Queen of Scots

195 [a] The Thracian Diomedes

196 [b] Hercules

197 [c] Brünnhilde

198 [b] James Watt

199 [b] Adrian Jones

200 [a] St Hippolytus

What's What?

201 [a] Anglo-Arab

202 [c] His kingdom

203 [a] Red

204 [b] British Eventing

205 [b] A type of horse-drawn carriage

206 [c] Cornish snaffle

207 [a] The pommel on a side-saddle that curves outwards over the rider's knee

208 [b] The start of the game when the umpire throws in the ball

209 [a] A Western girth

210 [b] A type of bit

211 [a] Halter class

212 [a] Shortened shoes designed to protect the toes of horses out at grass

213 [c] A painkiller

214 [a] In carriage driving, horses nearest to the vehicle

215 [b] They are all varieties of mounted game

216 [a] An iron base used for

217 [b] A tumour on the skin

218 [c] The offspring of a male ass and a female horse

219 [c] A variety of lucerne grown as a fodder crop

220 [b] Broke his neck

221 [b] A lasso

222 [a] Tungsten carbide

223 [c] A breaker-in or herder of horses

224 [b] A knight's warhorse

225 [b] White-capped breakers rolling in from the sea

226 [c] Someone who follows the hunt quietly on a rider's second horse until the fresh horse is needed

227 [b] Sign language used by bookmakers to communicate with each other

228 [b] Both have Grand National fences named after them

229 [b] A waterfall

230 [a] A breed of spotted horse from Denmark

231 [c] The quadrille performed by the Cadre Noir

232 [b] A standing martingale

233 [c] Let the buyer beware

234 [b] Leather bands through which the shafts of a vehicle pass to prevent it tipping up or down

235 [b] A type of noseband made of rubber

236 [c] A horse which has yet to win a race

238 [b] A jumping saddle

237 [c] A fast elevated four-beat gait

239 [b] The first volume of *The General Stud Book*

240 [c] A horny tumour on the inner surfaces of the wall of a horse's foot

241 [b] An involuntary snatching-up of the hind legs while a horse is walking

242 [a] A breed of horse with distinctive four-beat gaits

243 [c] A smooth gait in which the horse walks with his forelegs and trots behind

244 [b] Surgical shoes that extend backwards beyond the hoof

245 [a] Clip

246 [a] Shoulder-in

247 [b] Gardian

248 [a] He won the Grand National in 1931

249 [b] Horse of the river

250 [a] A complicated fracture of his near foreleg

251 [a] Horse sales

252 [b] Red

253 [c] A bacterium

254 [c] He became the only horse in Britain to race 100 times and never win

255 [a] 2 m (6.5 ft)

256 [a] The horse-drawn omnibus

257 [a] Edelweiss

258 [c] Stray animal

259 [a] A lightly built Thoroughbred horse lacking bone and substance

260 [a] A one-horse cart used in India

261 [a] Course for horses

262 [b] A Welsh/Arab cross

263 [b] A steam locomotive

264 [b] A hardy breed of horse originating in Russia

265 [a] 120–135 g (4.25–4.75 oz)

266 [a] Part of a Western saddle

267 [a] A white horse

268 [b] Stallion

269 [a] A Mexican lariat or lasso

270 [b] Tennessee Walking Horse

271 [b] Rings on a horse's harness through which the reins pass

272 [c] An Italian mounted herdsman

273 [c] Trained racehorses holding a licence in the name of her head lad

274 [b] A wooden board on an old type of saddle designed for women to rest their feet

275 [a] Cavalry saddles

276 [a] Morab

277 [a] To travel in a carriage squeezed in between two other people

278 [c] Fédération Équestre Internationale (FEI)

279 [c] Windsor

280 [c] To make it more lively be artifical means

281 [b] Shafts

282 [c] Ball

283 [b] A breed of horse found in Brazil

284 [c] USA Equestrian

285 [b] The crouching style of flat-race riding

286 [b] That by cantering a horse around a 13-metre diameter circle a rider could

balance on its croup
by centrifugal force

287 [c] Ox face

288 [b] A popular 19th-century
coaching song

289 [a] Fastenings which
secure the splinter
bar to the axle-
tree on a coach

290 [b] By giving it instructions
and turning a pin in
its ear it would carry
its rider anywhere

291 [a] The game of polo

292 [b] The gallows

293 [b] The arch which passes
over a horse's neck on
typical Russian harness

294 [c] The Pony Express
mail service

295 [b] The shield-shaped
bulge on the head of
an Arabian horse

296 [c] An attachment to a
harness racing bridle
to prevent a horse
spooking at shadows
on the ground

297 [a] A type of thin bit,
the forerunner of
the bridoon

298 [b] A trandem

299 [a] A non-handicap

300 [b] An overcoat worn
by coachmen

True or False?

301 True

302 True

303 False

304 True

305 False

306 True

307 False

308 True

309 True

310 False—they were Fell
ponies owned by
HM the Queen

311 True

312 False

313 False

314 True

315 False

316 True

317 True

318 False

319 True

320 False

321 True

322 False

323 False

324 False

325 False

326 True

327 True

328 True

329 False

330	True
331	False
332	True
333	True
334	False
335	True
336	True
337	False
338	True
339	False
340	True
341	True
342	False
343	True
344	True
345	False—she is his sister-in-law
346	True
347	False
348	True
349	True
350	True
351	False
352	True
353	False
354	True
355	True
356	True
357	False
358	False
359	True
360	True

361	True
362	True
363	False
364	True
365	True
366	True
367	False
368	False
369	True
370	True
371	False
372	True
373	True
374	True
375	False
376	True
377	True
378	True
379	False
380	True
381	True
382	True
383	False
384	True
385	False
386	False
387	False
388	False
389	True
390	False
391	True
392	False

393 False
394 True
395 True
396 True
397 True
398 True
399 False
400 False

How Many?

401 10 cm (4 in)
402 5
403 4
404 5: Dales, Fell, Exmoor, Dartmoor, New Forest
405 4: shooting, running, swimming, riding
406 18
407 10
408 Once
409 9
410 2
411 [b] 350
412 2
413 2: Badminton and Burghley
414 6: 4 in play and 2 substitutes
415 4
416 6: 1973, 1976, 1977, 1979, 1983, 1984
417 Twice (In 1990 and 1991)
418 2

419 3
420 3: light-, middle-, and heavyweight
421 4
422 [b] 150
423 4: Welsh Mountain Pony (Section A), Welsh Pony (Section B), Welsh Pony of Cob type (Section C), Welsh Cob (Section D)
424 4
425 3: dressage, eventing, show jumping
426 1
427 One fall incurs elimination
428 3: levade, courbette, capriole
429 2: passage, piaffe
430 45
431 2
432 2
433 8: C, M, B, F, A, K, E, H
434 7
435 3: 1964, 1965, 1966
436 9: 1954, 1957, 1960, 1968, 1970, 1972, 1976, 1977, 1983
437 2: one loose-ring jointed overcheck, one loose ring jointed bridoon
438 9–12
439 Two. Small hacks (148–154cm) and large hacks (154–160 cm)

440　4 seconds

441　[c] 210

442　4

443　5

444　3: 1980, 1994, 1996

445　12–20

446　3

447　2

448　5–6

449　Twice: 1956 in Stockholm and 1972 in Munich

450　3

451　6: Conversano, Favory, Maestoso, Neapolitano, Pluto, Siglavy

452　30

453　7

454　18

455　16

456　4

457　7: dressage, driving, endurance, eventing, reining, show jumping, vaulting

458　160 km /100 mi

459　37

460　3

461　3

462　Once: 1952 in Helsinki

463　5: blanket, frost, leopard, marble, snowflake

464　40

465　[b] 2–3

466　10–12

467　2

468　3: 2 wheelers, 1 leader

469　18 pairs

470　(a) 8

471　7

472　6: team, Tokyo in 1964; team, Mexico in 1968; team, Montreal in 1976; individual and team, Los Angeles in 1984; team, Seoul in 1988

473　9

474　Once (at three years old)

475　4

476　8

477　[b] Women

478　4

479　3

480　[c] 55 million

481　5: walk (fetgangur), trot (brökk), gallop (stökk), lateral pace (skeid), running walk (tölt)

482　4

　　In eventing: Charles Pahud de Mortanges (Holland), 1928 (Amsterdam) and 1932 (Los Angeles); Mark Todd (New Zealand), 1984 (Los Angeles) and 1988 (Seoul).

　　In dressage: Nicole Uphoff (Germany), 1988 (Seoul), 1992 (Barcelona).

In show jumping: Pierre Jonquères d'Oriola (France), 1952 (Helsinki) and 1964 (Tokyo).

483 One: Dawn Run (Champion Hurdle in 1984, Gold Cup in 1986)

484 2: the running and the flat-foot

485 Democratic Pary

486 8

487 46

488 2: overo, tobiano

489 5 kg (11 lb)

490 1–2 m / 1.09–2.19 yd

491 3: 1985, 1987, 1989

492 [b] 60

493 [c] 8 million

494 408 kg (900 lb)

495 16

496 10

497 [c] 1908

498 7.625 m (25 ft)

499 12: C, H, S, E, V, K, A, F, P, B, R, M

500 [b] 300–400

Which Horse?

501 [b] Charisma (in 1984 and 1988)

502 [a] Trakehner

503 [c] Cumberland Cobs

504 [a] The Cadre Noir

505 [c] Roan Barbary

506 [a] The Exmoor

507 [b] Rembrandt (in 1988 and 1992)

508 [b] Copenhagen (by the Duke of Wellington)

509 [b] A gift horse

510 [b] Softrack Skip Two Ramiro (with Guy Williams)

511 [b] Arkle

512 [b] Columbus

513 [c] Cob

514 [b] Stroller (the individual silver)

515 [b] Pony of the Americas

516 [c] Doublet

517 [b] Mon Mome, ridden by Liam Treadwell

518 [c] Cornishman V

519 [b] Eclipse

520 [c] White or grey

521 [c] Murphy Himself

522 [c] Fjord

523 [c] Shear L'Eau

524 [b] Danish Warmblood

525 [c] Criollo

526 [a] The Clydesdale

527 [b] Meteor (individual bronze, Helsinki, 1952; team gold, Stockholm, 1956; team gold, Rome, 1960)

528 [b] Man o' War
529 [c] The Akhal-Teke
530 [a] Golden Miller 1932-36
531 [c] The Saddlebred
532 [b] The Dales
533 [b] An international
          show jumper ridden
          by former Pony
          Club Chairman
          Dawn Wofford
          (née Palethorpe)
534 [b] Jaffa
535 [c] Midas Touch
536 [c] Satchmo
537 [b] Milton
538 [a] An English
          Thoroughbred stallion
          who became the
          foundation sire of
          the Standardbred
          racehorse
539 [b] Pacers
540 [b] Fell
541 [a] Copenhagen
542 [a] Lenamore
543 [a] The Arabian
544 [c] Bonfire
545 [b] The Camargue
546 [b] A racehorse
547 [a] Comanche
548 [c] Guzzle
549 [b] Kaimanawas
550 [a] Black Agnes

551 [b] The Criollo horses
          ridden by Aimé
          Tschiffely from
          Buenos Aires to
          Washington DC
552 [a] Justin Morgan
553 [c] The Icelandic
554 [b] Friesian
555 [a] The Hungarian-bred
          winner of the Epsom
          Derby in 1876
556 [a] Miner's Frolic
557 [a] Flying Childers
558 [b] Boomerang
559 [a] Xanthos
560 [a] The Shire
561 [b] The Caspian
562 [b] Dandy
563 [c] Gigolo (a Hanoverian)
564 [b] Missouri Fox
          Trotting Horse
565 [b] Boulonnais
566 [c] Sable Island
567 [a] Celer
568 [c] Corralero
569 [c] Shetland
570 [b] Camargue
571 [c] Star Appeal
572 [b] Noriker
573 [b] Hrimfaxi
574 [b] Billy
575 [a] Desert Orchid
576 [a] Boulonnais

577 [b] Stoney Crossing

578 [a] Canadian Horse

579 [c] Circus horses trained by Elizabeth, Empress of Austria

580 [b] Heatherbloom

581 [a] Gladiateur (in 1865)

582 [b] Crusier

583 [c] Never Say Die

584 [a] Highclere

585 [a] Holstein

586 [a] Connemara

587 [b] The first winner of the American Triple Crown (in 1919)

588 [b] Emilius (winner in 1823)

589 [b] The Emperor Hadrian

590 [c] Kabardin

591 [b] Jutland

592 [b] Percheron

593 [b] Lusitano

594 [c] Trotters

595 [a] Merely-a-Monarch

596 [c] Desert Orchid

597 [b] Bonite

598 [c] Kincsem

599 [a] Laura Bechtolsheimer

600 [c] R.O. Grand Sultan

Sporting Chance

601 [c] 14.2 hh (148 cm)

602 [a] A type of show jumping fence

603 [b] Dressage

604 [c] Competitors at Badminton Horse Trials

605 [a] 4 years old

606 [b] 10

607 [b] 6

608 [a] Jenny Pitman

609 [c] 8 minutes

610 [b] Endurance riding

611 [a] 2

612 [a] Carriage driving

613 [a] Dressage

614 [b] Medium and free

615 [b] Fairly good

616 [b] A driving competition

617 [a] Bruce Davidson

618 [b] A mounted game

619 [a] A dressage rider

620 [c] On an eventing cross-country course

621 [c] Hickstead

622 [c] Horseball

623 [c] 4

624 [a] In a dressage arena

625 [c] A narrow cross-country fence

626 [c] At least 7-years-old

627 [c] 4: medium, free, extended, collected

628 [c] Great Britain

629 [b] 7–10 yd (6.4–9.1 m)

630 [a] 1957

631 [b] Reining

632 [c] The trail of the fox

633 [a] Show jumping

634 [c] A competition for leisure riders comprising orienteering, basic riding control and cross-country

635 [a] The British Jumping Derby at Hickstead

636 [b] Polo

637 [b] 12–16

638 [a] Ulla Salzgeber and Rusty

639 [c] Elementary

640 [a] 10 (in some tests, such as Pony Club horse trials, the rider mark is doubled)

641 [c] Polo

642 [c] Doncaster

643 [c] The rider is eliminated

644 [c] It was declared void because of a false start

645 [b] 2

646 [b] Polo

647 [b] An obstacle on the Burghley Horse Trials cross-country course

648 [b] Aintree

649 [a] Numbers 1 and 2

650 [a] Meriel Naughton (on 30 January 1976)

651 [c] Caroline Bradley (in 1978)

652 [a] King Charles II

653 [b] The Aga Khan

654 [b] Right

655 [b] Atlanta in 1996

656 [c] Cynthia Haydon

657 [a] Cheltenham Races

658 [b] Non-commissioned military officers

659 [a] Western riding

660 [b] Team gold medallist Gillian Rolton on Peppermint Grove (Australian team)

661 [c] Hickstead (England beat USA 15–9)

662 [b] France

663 [a] 5 furlongs

664 [b] Diana Thorne (on 7 February 1976)

665 [b] A rider who completes Badminton Horse Trials five times

666 [c] Fishing

667 [b] A hound who has not finished one cub-hunting season

668 [c] Power and speed

669 [b] Charisma (in Auckland in 1990)

670 [c] Germany

671 [c] William Fox-Pitt (Badminton, Burghley, Kentucky, Luhmühlen)

672 [a] A 6-metre circle

673 [c] Jane Holderness-Roddam (née Bullen) (in Mexico in 1968)

674 [a] A hound who cuts corners instead of following the true line of a fox

675 [a] The Whitakers of Great Britain (John, Michael, Robert, Louise (at Drammen, in Norway))

676 [b] Wendell T. Robie

677 [b] Phar Lap

678 [a] Nelson Pessoa (of Brazil, in Lucerne in 1966)

679 [c] Markus Fuchs

680 [a] US$ 10,000,000

681 [b] Ballycotton (1990 to 1995, and 1997)

682 [b] L'Escargot

683 [a] Richard Meade (at the 1972 Olympic Games in Munich. This was the last international three-day event in which bonus points could be gained on the steeplechase and cross-country)

684 [b] A famous harness raceway at Lexington, in Kentucky

685 [c] First rider to win Burghley Horse Trials four years running

686 [b] Franke Sloothaak on Leonardo (at Chaudfontaine in Belgium)

687 [a] Jimmy Hill

688 [c] Chris Collins (on Stephen's Society)

689 [b] Sunsalve (ridden by Elizabeth Anderson he won the Queen's Cup in 1957; ridden by David Broome he won the King's Cup in 1960)

690 [c] Once every four years in the year before the Olympic Games

691 [b] Lana Dupont (in Tokyo in 1964: she was a member of the United States team which won a silver medal)

692 [b] Harness racing

693 [a] Harness racing

694 [b] Sue Benson

695 [b] Dorian Williams

696 [c] Rollback

697 [a] Richard Dunwoody

698 [c] Marion Mould (on Stroller in 1970

699 [a] 3

700 [b] Paul Sidwell

Where?

701 [b] By his shoulder, facing his tail

702 [b] Gatcombe

703 [b] On his lower jaw

704 [b] Outside of the leg

705 [c] On a stable door

706 [b] On the heel of a horse's forefoot

707 [c] On the joint capsules of a horse's hock

708 [b] In mid-stream

709 [a] On a Pelham bridle with a single rein

710 [c] At the back of his fetlock joint

711 [c] From Ghent to Aix

712 [a] Hickstead

713 [b] Ireland

714 [b] Stoneleigh

715 [c] On the girth straps of your saddle

716 [c] Kentucky

717 [b] Behind his fetlock joints

718 [c] Round a horse's neck

719 [c] On a bridle with a curb chain

720 [b] On a pair of riding boots

721 [b] On a horse's lower legs

722 [c] On stirrup irons

723 [c] On his legs

724 [c] On a show jumping course

725 [b] In British state processions

726 [a] A horse's large intestines

727 [a] On the horse's hoof, from the wearing surface upwards

728 [b] In Northants.

729 [c] On the take-off side of a practice fence

730 [c] Warendorf

731 [a] On the outside of the fence, furthest away from the horse

732 [c] On a horse's neck (it is a pronounced dimple mark, believed to be a sign of luck)

733 [a] To the headcollar of a stabled horse to prevent him biting his clothing

734 [a] It is a by-product of wheat

735 [c] Warwickshire

736 [c] In his stifle

737 [c] Exmoor

738 [a] Newmarket

739 [a] On a harness horse

740 [b] Thirlestane Castle

741 [b] In his hind leg

742 [c] In West Somerset and North East Devon

743 [c] Up to bed

744 [c] On a horse's hind quarters

745 [c] Mongolia

746 [b] Between his ears

747 [b] On a curb chain (the lip strap passes through it)

748 [a] Stoneleigh

749 [a] Wembley Arena

750 [c] On a horseshoe

751 [b] Normandy

752 [a] On a Western saddle

753 [b] In his tail

754 [c] Ayr

755 [a] On a horse's fetlocks and pasterns

756 [c] In County Cork (from Buttevant Church to the spire of St Leger Church)

757 [a] On a horse-drawn vehicle (it is a stiff bar, at the front of a vehicle, by which it is drawn)

758 [c] Rome

759 [a] In the hunting field (a pack is 'all on' when every hound comprising it is present)

760 [a] Newmarket

761 [b] Surrounding his coronet

762 [c] Sussex

763 [a] In his mouth

764 [b] Saumur

765 [b] On a stirrup leather

766 [c] On a horse's teeth

767 [b] Rome

768 [a] At the back of his knee

769 [c] From London to York

770 [a] Norfolk

771 [c] Dublin

772 [b] Balaclava

773 [a] Canada (they are the Canadian stretch of the Niagara Falls)

774 [b] In his forearm

775 [c] The First World War

776 [a] Aachen

777 [b] Alberta, in Canada

778 [c] In Siberia [in the Altai Mountains]

779 [a] Switzerland

780 [c] In India

781 [b] Stockholm

782 [a] Where his horse's hoof had stepped

783 [c] In the New Forest (agisters supervise the welfare of all ponies and other animals turned out on the Forest)

784 [a] Being driven in tandem behind his stablemate Xerxes

785 [a] Oakham, in Rutland

786 [c] On a horse's breast and flanks

787 [b] Longchamp

788 [c] Revelation

789 [b] Opposite the Royal Exchange in London

790 [a] Churchill Downs

791 [a] The Lakes of Killarney

792 [c] The Dormello Stud in Italy

793 [c] Persia

794 [c] Under their saddles

795 [c] About 30° north and south

796 [c] Sweden

797 [b] On a draught horse's collar

798 [a] Between St Joseph in Missouri and Sacramento in California

799 [a] On a farrier's anvil

800 [b] Iceland

How and Why?

801 [a] By the appearance of his teeth

802 [a] Sliced lengthways

803 [c] 122 cm (4 ft)

804 [c] They are likely to cause colic

805 [b] Move his leg and watch for signs of pain

806 [a] The horse has to eat in an unnatural position

807 [c] So that the horse makes equal use of the muscles on both sides of his body

808 [b] Well soaked in water

809 [b] They ingest and destroy parasites that are harmful to horses

810 [c] The hair is a natural protection against flies, parasites and foreign objects

811 [c] Fit a fillet string

812 [b] They contain banned substances

813 [c] Put your knuckles on the stirrup bar of the saddle and adjust the leathers so that the irons reach your armpit

814 [b] To prevent your saddle from slipping forwards

815 [a] It has fixed cheeks

816 [a] Because that is when the biting midges which cause it are most active

817 [a] You cannot get out of the way quickly if he moves

818 [c] To protect your hands

against rope burns

819 [b] On all four legs over a layer of padding

820 [c] They can cause serious injury if they become entangled

821 [c] Two fingers' width below the projecting cheek bones

822 [b] It might shrink and restrict his blood circulation

823 [b] As for eventing cross-country

824 [a] Dappled

825 [c] Walk beside him and turn him away from you so that you stay on his outside

826 [c] To prevent the rider's stick getting caught up

827 [c] Give the horse toys to play with

828 [c] So the horse won't anticipate the movements

829 [c] It helps to reduce worm infestation

830 [c] It helps to prevent the horse's mouth becoming one-sided

831 [c] By fitting a shoe with a short, narrow inner heel

832 [b] The quality of the summer coat will be poor

833 [a] His hip will drop when his sound limb strikes the ground

834 [b] To prevent it pressing on the horse's backbone

835 [a] The horse has a sore throat and finds it difficult to swallow

836 [b] Because they are ill or in pain

837 [c] By holding up a foreleg

838 [b] The coffin bone

839 [c] Rat-catcher

840 [b] With a sweat-scraper

841 [c] Go back to grid work

842 [b] A horse might get his feet tangled in it

843 [a] To protect a horse's head when travelling

844 [a] Your reins will slip through them

845 [b] To see a fine lady upon a white horse

846 [c] To protect him from overreach injuries

847 [a] A brace

848 [b] To listen to a horse's heart, lungs and gut

849 [b] Broken-kneed

850 [a] Snip

851 [b] Pinch a fold of skin on his neck and see if it springs back to normal within a second

852 [b] School him over crossed-pole fences to steer him towards the middle

853 [a] It exerts pressure on the horse's nose

854 [a] To lead a strong horse, particularly one who is inclined to rear

855 [b] It transfers weight from the heels on to the frog

856 [a] They are inclined to be weak

857 [b] You will unbalance the horse

858 [c] Because the horse judges his take-off point from the ground-line

859 [c] Point it towards his shoulder

860 [b] He introduced the forward seat

861 [b] Attach a lunge-rein to the side of the vehicle and use it to apply pressure above his hocks

862 [a], [b] and [c]

863 [b] By raising his whip or hand

864 [b] Riding on a pony

865 [c] Also ran

866 [a] Snowflake

867 [c] To give extra grip in muddy ground

868 [b] A CIC is a one-day event, a CCI is a three-day event

869 [a] They place undue strain on the ligaments at the back of the carpus

870 [c] To replace body salts lost during strenuous exercise

871 [c] Contraction of the tendons of the digital flexors

872 [a] For its ancient, well-preserved cave paintings of horses

873 [a] To prevent them injuring themselves with their studs when they fold their front legs

874 [b] A horse can see almost all round himself without turning his head

875 [b] Because it was once believed that the tree's seeds would cure a broken-winded horse

876 [a] It has horseshoe-shaped pods

877 [b] It is clear and

straw-coloured,
like thin honey

878 [b] They are named
after the Mexican
Count de Palomino
who was presented
with a gold-coloured
horse by the Spanish
explorer, Cortés

879 [a] She became the first
British rider to win a
dressage medal (riding
Dutch Courage she
won the individual
bronze at the World
Championships)

880 [a] Her horse, Toytown,
was injured in training

881 [b] Buffalo Bill

882 [c] An iron chair used
to be placed by the
jump for the distance
judge to sit on

883 [a] Mounted on a
Thoroughbred

884 [a] It aids the correct
functioning of muscle,
bone, teeth and
enzyme systems

885 [b] The hell of horses

886 [b] In German

887 [c] By eight horses

888 [b] Two (initially riding for
Great Britain, he opted
to represent Ireland in
1992, before switching
his loyalties back to
Great Britain in 2007)

889 [c] As a stage coachman

890 [b] They are all left-handed

891 [b] A parasite beneath
the skin caused
slight bleeding
which coloured the
horses' sweat

892 [b] They invented the
breast harness

893 [c] Madly off in all
directions

894 [c] To provide milk
and meat

895 [c] On foot

896 [a] To protect his chest
in battle (it was
a breastplate, an
important part of
horse armour)

897 [c] By raising his whip
hand to face-level

898 [b] It was the first year
in which mounted
horsemen competed
in races at the
Olympic Games

899 [a] Thiamine (vitamin B₁)

900 [b] They are said to be
based on the letters
used on the stable yard
walls at the old Imperial
German Court

Mixed Bag

901 [a] The bridoon strap on a double bridle

902 [b] There is no forward movement in piaffe

903 [a] When a horse's hind feet step beyond the hoofprints of his forefeet

904 [c] A horse who holds his head very high

905 [c] On the bottom of a stable door

906 [c] Being run away with

907 [c] The liver

908 [a] The Royal Canadian Mounted Police

909 [c] A tumour of the skin

910 [b] A plaited leather girth

911 [a] A term used to describe a groove in the ground surface of a horseshoe

912 [b] Loops on saddlery through which straps are passed

913 [b] Fastenings at the ends of reins and cheek pieces

914 [c] A body protector

915 [a] Monty Roberts

916 [c] A gold-coloured under-blanket with black and red stripes

917 [a] First cervical vertebra

918 [b] Buckle guard

919 [b] A rider who sits on the back of the saddle with his legs pushed forward

920 [b] Pippa Funnell on Supreme Rock

921 [b] Stainless steel

922 [a] Cross-over reins attached to the saddle to prevent a pony putting his head down to graze

923 [c] Tetanus

924 [b] A horse who brushes

925 [a] A mechanical device for exercising horses

926 [c] A cross between a male zebra and a female horse

927 [b] A Puissance

928 [a] A defect of the wall of the hoof

929 [b] Royal Horse Artillery

930 [b] To reverse the natural or proper order of things

931 [a] The White Knight

932 [c] Riding for the Disabled Association

933 [c] A cow pony trained to 'cut out' selected animals from a herd

934 [b] Immersing a horse's injured foot in warm water

935 [c] On a mouthing bit

936 [b] False bones caused by hardening of the cartilages of the pedal bones

937 [b] The rounded shape of a jumping horse as he clears the summit of an obstacle

938 [c] A few inches below the point of his hock

939 [b] 7.5–8.5%

940 [a] A thorough grooming of a horse

941 [b] A device fitted around the mouthpiece of a bit to prevent chafing

942 [c] A type of curb bit

943 [b] Unrefined black treacle

944 [a] FBHS (Fellow of the British Horse Society)

945 [a] Nicholas Evans

946 [a] A shoe has become loose

947 [c] A horseshoe nail

948 [c] Rest and anti-inflammatory drugs

949 [b] A cross between a zebra and a donkey

950 [c] Nettle rash

951 [c] Daisy Baker

952 [b] Inflammation of the cornea of the eye

953 [a] Tutankhamen's (in The Cairo Museum, in Egypt)

954 [b] Touch of Class and Joe Fargis (America's team and individual gold medallists in Los Angeles in 1984)

955 [b] A type of safety stirrup-iron

956 [c] Leap of the goat

957 [b] A tick-borne equine disease causing fever and weakness

958 [c] One cast from the near-hind leg of a grey mare

959 [a] A pair of blinkers with a slit in each eye shield

960 [b] A barge horse

961 [c] An American cavalry general

962 [c] A white horse

963 [b] R.S. Surtees in *Mr Sponge's Sporting Tour*

964 [a] The first milk produced by a mare after she has given birth to a foal

965 [b] A horse cut into a chalk hillside in Oxfordshire

966 [c] *International Velvet*

967 [b] Mary Stewart

968 [b] A carriage horse let out for hire to the public

969 [c] Grass Sickness

970 [c] Dishing

971 [a] Plaited cotton cord reins

972 [b] The hard palate

973 [a] A famous 19th-century maker of bits

974 [a] A hoax or fraud

975 [c] Sore shins

976 [a] An exceptionally hardy breed of horse living in northern Siberia

977 [b] John Byng, Viscount Torrington

978 [c] Having long teeth

979 [a] Streptococcus equi

980 [b] The eating of dung

981 [c] Lanfranco 'Frankie' Dettori (at Chepstow on 27 August 1990, at the age of 19)

982 [b] (Frederic) Remington was an American painter and sculptor

983 [a] Handel

984 [c] Both are in the shape of a figure-of-eight

985 [b] Henry Wadsworth Longfellow

986 [b] A military saddle cloth

987 [b] Turner

988 [a] 1927

989 [a] Stadhampton, in Oxfordshire

990 [b] The liver fluke

991 [b] *The Tales of a Grandfather* (the perpetrators of the crime had the same done to them before being executed)

992 [c] If only you have the money, you can do anything

993 [b] Running Rein

994 [a] Anthony Trollope

995 [b] A covered, horse-drawn wagon used by pioneers crossing the North American prairies

996 [c] 40 mph

997 [b] 42 (the Australian gelding Tango Duke, foaled in 1935, died on 30 January 1978)

998 [b] *Jamaica Inn* by Daphne du Maurier

999 [c] French ridden trotting racing

1000 [a] The English Cart Horse Society

1001 [a] Fennel-flavoured gingerbread